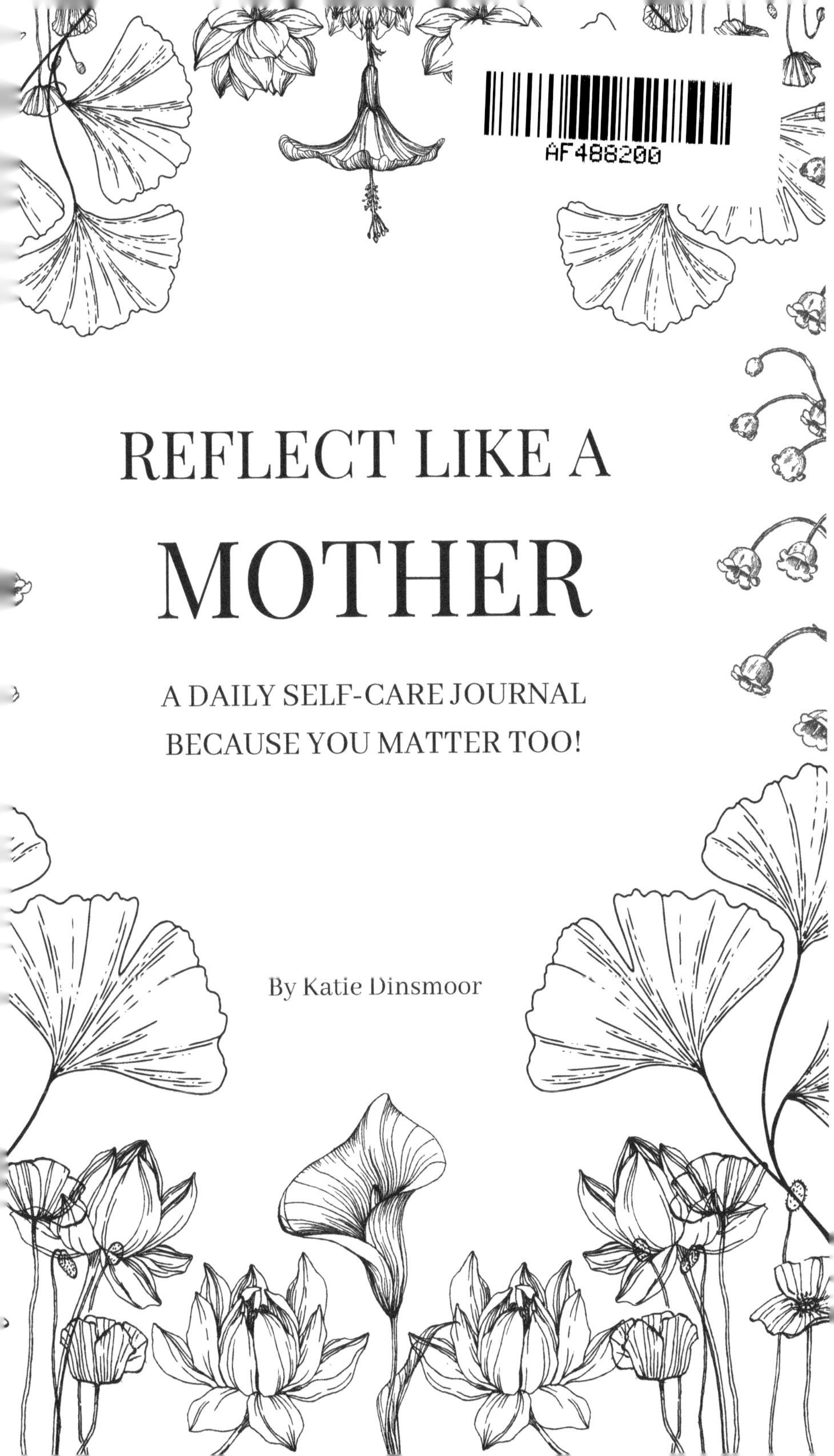

REFLECT LIKE A
MOTHER

A DAILY SELF-CARE JOURNAL
BECAUSE YOU MATTER TOO!

By Katie Dinsmoor

Live Your Flow Press
Stanford, CA/USA 94305

Ordering Information:
Quantity sales. Special discounts are available on quantity purchases by corporations, associations, and others. For details, contact the "Special Sales Department" at the address above.

Reflect Like A Mother / Katie Dinsmoor —1st ed.
ISBN 9798987962800

This book is dedicated to all the
Moms. Thank you, you know why.
And for the ones who bring joy and
light, my shining daughter and son,
thank you for making me a Mom.

WELCOME,
YOU MAGNIFICENT MOTHER!

NOW SIT BACK AND RELAX. CONGRATULATE YOURSELF ON BEING RIGHT WHERE YOU ARE AND TAKING THIS NEXT STEP ON YOUR SELF-CARE JOURNEY.

Being a mother is incredibly hard! You do so much! You are constantly on-call working; there is no time off, unpaid overtime is a constant, and the day-to-day tasks can feel endless. It is truly the most demanding job out there. Even if you get a little time for yourself, your mind doesn't turn off easily. There are endless to-do lists, upcoming projects to oversee, and worries floating around monopolizing your mental space. "Mom brains" are always working and it is exhausting. Sometimes we might wonder where that pre-mom self is buried. Is she still in there, hopeful, self-confident, clear-headed and well-rested? We may never be that exact same version of ourselves again, but now we are so much more!

Perhaps you didn't' fully realize the personal transformation that would take place when joining the motherhood tribe. Transformation is hard. Let's embrace and celebrate this beautiful new version of yourself. She might be covered in baby food, hair unwashed for several days, and wearing the same comfy sweats she slept in the night before, but she is killing it! You have created life. You are sustaining life. You can grow and nourish new little humans in this world. You can still grow and nourish yourself too!

Motherhood allows us a brilliant opportunity to reconnect with ourselves in a new way. We get to learn more about our authentic selves, what truly matters to us, and what we want our life to be. Your future vision of yourself starts now. Right where you are is exactly where you should be. You are the most perfect version of you. Everything in your pre-mom self has been masterfully integrated into the brilliant whole person you are in this moment. You are not only a magnificent Mom, but a stunning, one-of-a-kind, irreplaceable, magical being that deserves just as much love and care as your darling babies. It's okay to baby yourself a bit too. You have never needed a little TLC more!

It's easy to feel like we don't have time for ourselves when we are constantly on the work clock that is motherhood. The thought of adding self-care to our daily to-do list might seem overwhelming. It can sometimes feel like self-care is just another thing we are failing to fit in. This journal is meant to simplify self-care and make it not only easily manageable, but even a little fun. By taking 10 or 15 minutes each evening to self-reflect, you can nourish the unique, perfect splendor that is YOU!

ABOUT USING THIS JOURNAL

TAKE A LONG DEEP BREATH. USING THIS DAILY JOURNAL IS SUPER SIMPLE. HERE ARE A FEW IDEAS AND SUGGESTIONS ON MAKING IT WORK FOR YOU.

This journal consists of 66 days of self-care reflections. There is not a definitive amount of time it takes for every person to successful develop a new habit; but most research concurs that somewhere around 66 days is a good ballpark. This allows enough time to incorporate a self-care ritual into your daily routines.

The journal is designed to be brief, simple, and repetitive so each night you'll have the opportunity to give yourself a few moments of undivided focus. It's okay to be selfish for ten minutes! There is no pressure to fill out all the sections and there is no right or wrong way to approach the daily reflections. The primary purpose is to give yourself some much deserved attention.

At the end of the journal, you will find a few blank pages for additional notes. You can reflect on how integrating this journal into your daily routine went for you. You can note any patterns that arose or thoughts / feelings that the process evoked.

In addition, you'll find a section called Daily Doodle Directives. This is an index you can refer to if you'd like some inspiration for your Daily Doodles. There are 66 different prompts.

Feel free to go straight down the list and use one for each day, pick and choose certain prompts that resonate with you that day, or just free doodle if your heart desires! You can simply fill the Daily Doodle page with a color to represent your mood that day, a word to summarize your overall feeling, write yourself a sweet little note, or draw / write anything that feels cathartic to you in the moment. Let your creativity flow and follow your instincts. The Daily Doodle Directives are there if you want the guidance, but are not meant to be instructions.

Take what works and leave what doesn't. There are no rules- except you must read the daily affirmation to yourself and do your best to accept it as truth :) Know your unique value and worth! You are irreplaceable! So let's start taking care of YOU!

LET'S BEGIN.

You are exactly where you are
supposed to be.

DAILY DOODLE & AFFIRMATION

DATE :

I am enough!

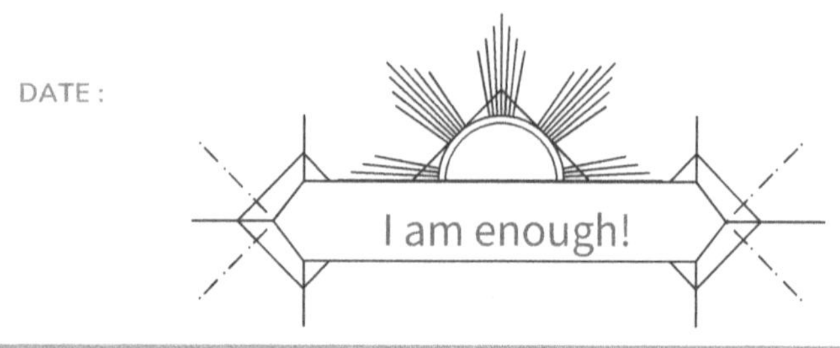

SELF-CARE REFLECTIONS

DATE :   M T W T F S S

DID I SET AN INTENTION FOR THE DAY? Y / N

TODAY'S ACCOMPLISHMENTS
BIG OR SMALL

1

2

3

BODY

CUPS OF WATER DRANK: _____

HOURS SLEPT LAST NIGHT: _____

MINUTES SPENT EXERCISING: _____

WHAT I ATE TODAY NOURISHED & ENERGIZED ME? Y / N

DIETARY NOTES: _____________

____

ONE WORD TO DESCRIBE HOW I FELT PHYSICALLY TODAY WAS ______________.

SOUL

DID I FEEL HOPEFUL TODAY? Y / N

MINUTES SPENT ON MEDITATIVE ACTIVITY OR IN A STATE OF FLOW: _____

ONE THING THAT GAVE ME PURPOSE TODAY WAS ______

____

____

SOMETHING I STRUGGLED WITH TODAY WAS ____________

____

____

MIND

WAS MY SELF-TALK TODAY KIND & COMPASSIONATE? Y / N

ONE THING I APPRECIATE ABOUT MYSELF IS ________________

____

SOMETHING I'M GRATEFUL FOR TODAY WAS ______________

____

____

DAILY DOODLE & Affirmation

SELF-CARE REFLECTIONS

DATE :   M T W T F S S

DID I SET AN INTENTION FOR THE DAY? Y / N

TODAY'S ACCOMPLISHMENTS
BIG OR SMALL

1

2

3

BODY

CUPS OF WATER DRANK: _____
HOURS SLEPT LAST NIGHT: _____
MINUTES SPENT EXERCISING: _____
WHAT I ATE TODAY NOURISHED & ENERGIZED ME? Y / N

DIETARY NOTES: ____________
____
ONE WORD TO DESCRIBE HOW I FELT PHYSICALLY TODAY WAS ______________.

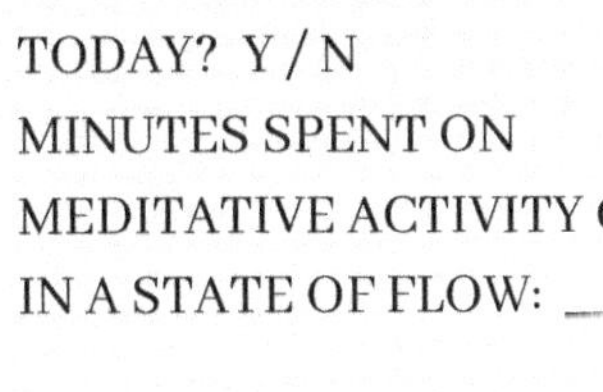

SOUL

DID I FEEL HOPEFUL TODAY? Y / N
MINUTES SPENT ON MEDITATIVE ACTIVITY OR IN A STATE OF FLOW: ___

ONE THING THAT GAVE ME PURPOSE TODAY WAS ______
____
____

SOMETHING I STRUGGLED WITH TODAY WAS ____________
____
____

MIND

WAS MY SELF-TALK TODAY KIND & COMPASSIONATE? Y / N

ONE THING I APPRECIATE ABOUT MYSELF IS _______________
____

SOMETHING I'M GRATEFUL FOR TODAY WAS _______________
____
____

DAILY DOODLE & AFFIRMATION

DATE :

I shine!

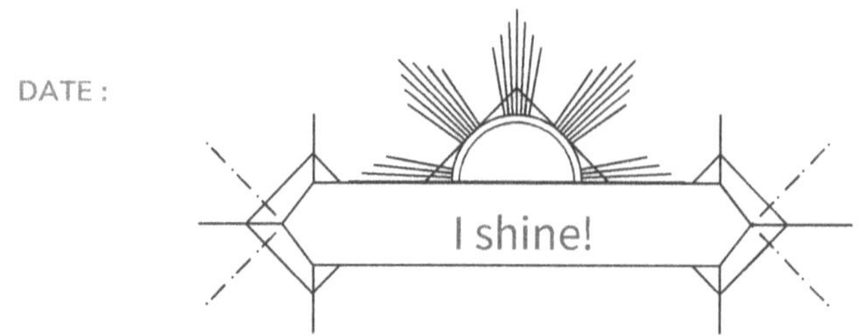

SELF-CARE REFLECTIONS

DATE: M T W T F S S

DID I SET AN INTENTION FOR THE DAY? Y / N

TODAY'S ACCOMPLISHMENTS
BIG OR SMALL

1
2
3

BODY

CUPS OF WATER DRANK: _____
HOURS SLEPT LAST NIGHT: _____
MINUTES SPENT EXERCISING: _____
WHAT I ATE TODAY NOURISHED & ENERGIZED ME? Y / N

DIETARY NOTES: ___________
____
ONE WORD TO DESCRIBE HOW I FELT PHYSICALLY TODAY WAS ______________.

SOUL

DID I FEEL HOPEFUL TODAY? Y / N
MINUTES SPENT ON MEDITATIVE ACTIVITY OR IN A STATE OF FLOW: _____

ONE THING THAT GAVE ME PURPOSE TODAY WAS ______
____
____

SOMETHING I STRUGGLED WITH TODAY WAS ___________
____
____

MIND

WAS MY SELF-TALK TODAY KIND & COMPASSIONATE? Y / N

ONE THING I APPRECIATE ABOUT MYSELF IS _______________
____

SOMETHING I'M GRATEFUL FOR TODAY WAS _______________
____
____

DAILY DOODLE & AFFIRMATION

DATE :

SELF-CARE REFLECTIONS

DATE :   M T W T F S S

DID I SET AN INTENTION FOR THE DAY? Y / N

TODAY'S ACCOMPLISHMENTS
BIG OR SMALL

1

2

3

BODY

CUPS OF WATER DRANK: _____

HOURS SLEPT LAST NIGHT: _____

MINUTES SPENT EXERCISING: _____

WHAT I ATE TODAY NOURISHED & ENERGIZED ME? Y / N

DIETARY NOTES: _____________
____

ONE WORD TO DESCRIBE HOW I FELT PHYSICALLY TODAY WAS _____________.

SOUL

DID I FEEL HOPEFUL TODAY? Y / N

MINUTES SPENT ON MEDITATIVE ACTIVITY OR IN A STATE OF FLOW: _____

ONE THING THAT GAVE ME PURPOSE TODAY WAS _______
____
____

SOMETHING I STRUGGLED WITH TODAY WAS _____________
____
____

MIND

WAS MY SELF-TALK TODAY KIND & COMPASSIONATE? Y / N

ONE THING I APPRECIATE ABOUT MYSELF IS _____________________
____

SOMETHING I'M GRATEFUL FOR TODAY WAS _______________
____
____

DAILY DOODLE & AFFIRMATION

DATE :

SELF-CARE REFLECTIONS

DATE :   M T W T F S S

DID I SET AN INTENTION FOR THE DAY? Y / N

TODAY'S ACCOMPLISHMENTS
BIG OR SMALL

1
2
3

BODY

CUPS OF WATER DRANK: ______
HOURS SLEPT LAST NIGHT: ______
MINUTES SPENT EXERCISING: ______
WHAT I ATE TODAY NOURISHED &
ENERGIZED ME? Y / N

DIETARY NOTES: ______________
____
ONE WORD TO DESCRIBE
HOW I FELT PHYSICALLY
TODAY WAS ________________.

SOUL

DID I FEEL HOPEFUL
TODAY? Y / N
MINUTES SPENT ON
MEDITATIVE ACTIVITY OR
IN A STATE OF FLOW: ______

ONE THING THAT GAVE ME
PURPOSE TODAY WAS ______
____
____

SOMETHING I STRUGGLED
WITH TODAY WAS ___________
____
____

MIND

WAS MY SELF-TALK TODAY KIND
& COMPASSIONATE? Y / N

ONE THING I APPRECIATE ABOUT
MYSELF IS ____________________
____

SOMETHING I'M GRATEFUL FOR
TODAY WAS __________________
____
____

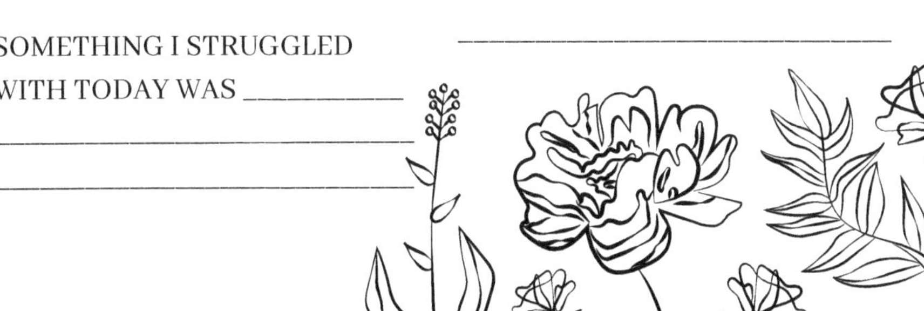

DAILY DOODLE & AFFIRMATION

DATE :

SELF-CARE REFLECTIONS

M T W T F S S

DID I SET AN INTENTION FOR THE DAY? Y / N

TODAY'S ACCOMPLISHMENTS
BIG OR SMALL

1

2

3

BODY

CUPS OF WATER DRANK: _____
HOURS SLEPT LAST NIGHT: _____
MINUTES SPENT EXERCISING: _____
WHAT I ATE TODAY NOURISHED & ENERGIZED ME? Y / N

DIETARY NOTES: ______________
____
ONE WORD TO DESCRIBE HOW I FELT PHYSICALLY TODAY WAS _______________.

SOUL

DID I FEEL HOPEFUL TODAY? Y / N
MINUTES SPENT ON MEDITATIVE ACTIVITY OR IN A STATE OF FLOW: _____

ONE THING THAT GAVE ME PURPOSE TODAY WAS ______
____
____

SOMETHING I STRUGGLED WITH TODAY WAS ____________
____
____

MIND

WAS MY SELF-TALK TODAY KIND & COMPASSIONATE? Y / N

ONE THING I APPRECIATE ABOUT MYSELF IS _________________
____

SOMETHING I'M GRATEFUL FOR TODAY WAS ________________
____
____

DAILY DOODLE & AFFIRMATION

DATE :

SELF-CARE REFLECTIONS

DATE : M T W T F S S

DID I SET AN INTENTION FOR THE DAY? Y / N

TODAY'S ACCOMPLISHMENTS
BIG OR SMALL

1

2

3

BODY

CUPS OF WATER DRANK: _____
HOURS SLEPT LAST NIGHT: _____
MINUTES SPENT EXERCISING: _____
WHAT I ATE TODAY NOURISHED & ENERGIZED ME? Y / N

DIETARY NOTES: ____________
____
ONE WORD TO DESCRIBE HOW I FELT PHYSICALLY TODAY WAS ____________.

SOUL

DID I FEEL HOPEFUL TODAY? Y / N
MINUTES SPENT ON MEDITATIVE ACTIVITY OR IN A STATE OF FLOW: _____

ONE THING THAT GAVE ME PURPOSE TODAY WAS _____
____
____

SOMETHING I STRUGGLED WITH TODAY WAS ____________
____
____

MIND

WAS MY SELF-TALK TODAY KIND & COMPASSIONATE? Y / N

ONE THING I APPRECIATE ABOUT MYSELF IS ____________
____

SOMETHING I'M GRATEFUL FOR TODAY WAS ____________
____
____

DAILY DOODLE & AFFIRMATION

DATE :

I am smart!

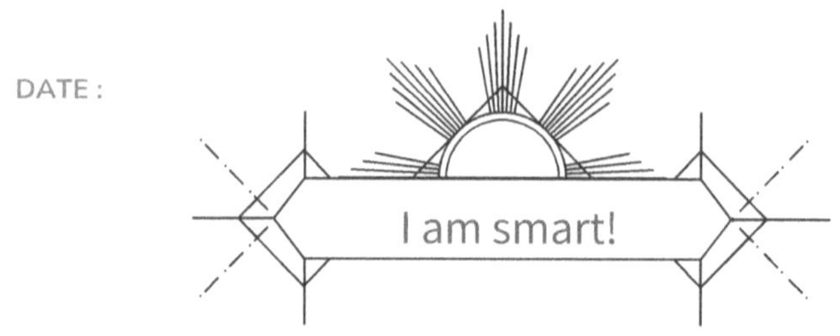

SELF-CARE REFLECTIONS

DATE : M T W T F S S

DID I SET AN INTENTION FOR THE DAY? Y / N

TODAY'S ACCOMPLISHMENTS
BIG OR SMALL

1
2
3

BODY

CUPS OF WATER DRANK: _____
HOURS SLEPT LAST NIGHT: _____
MINUTES SPENT EXERCISING: _____
WHAT I ATE TODAY NOURISHED &
ENERGIZED ME? Y / N

DIETARY NOTES: _____________
____
ONE WORD TO DESCRIBE
HOW I FELT PHYSICALLY
TODAY WAS _______________.

SOUL

DID I FEEL HOPEFUL
TODAY? Y / N
MINUTES SPENT ON
MEDITATIVE ACTIVITY OR
IN A STATE OF FLOW: ______

ONE THING THAT GAVE ME
PURPOSE TODAY WAS ______
____
____

SOMETHING I STRUGGLED
WITH TODAY WAS _____________
____
____

MIND

WAS MY SELF-TALK TODAY KIND
& COMPASSIONATE? Y / N

ONE THING I APPRECIATE ABOUT
MYSELF IS _____________________
____

SOMETHING I'M GRATEFUL FOR
TODAY WAS __________________
____
____

DAILY DOODLE & AFFIRMATION

DATE :

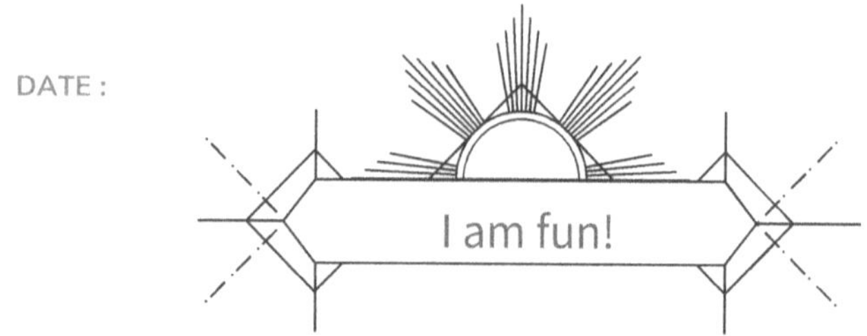

SELF-CARE REFLECTIONS

DATE: _______________   M T W T F S S

DID I SET AN INTENTION FOR THE DAY? Y / N

____

____

____

TODAY'S ACCOMPLISHMENTS
BIG OR SMALL

1 _________________________________

2 _________________________________

3 _________________________________

BODY

CUPS OF WATER DRANK: _____

HOURS SLEPT LAST NIGHT: _____

MINUTES SPENT EXERCISING: _____

WHAT I ATE TODAY NOURISHED & ENERGIZED ME? Y / N

DIETARY NOTES: ______________

____

ONE WORD TO DESCRIBE HOW I FELT PHYSICALLY TODAY WAS ______________.

SOUL

DID I FEEL HOPEFUL TODAY? Y / N

MINUTES SPENT ON MEDITATIVE ACTIVITY OR IN A STATE OF FLOW: _____

ONE THING THAT GAVE ME PURPOSE TODAY WAS _____

____

____

SOMETHING I STRUGGLED WITH TODAY WAS ____________

____

____

MIND

WAS MY SELF-TALK TODAY KIND & COMPASSIONATE? Y / N

ONE THING I APPRECIATE ABOUT MYSELF IS ____________________

____

SOMETHING I'M GRATEFUL FOR TODAY WAS ________________

____

____

DAILY DOODLE & Affirmation

DATE :

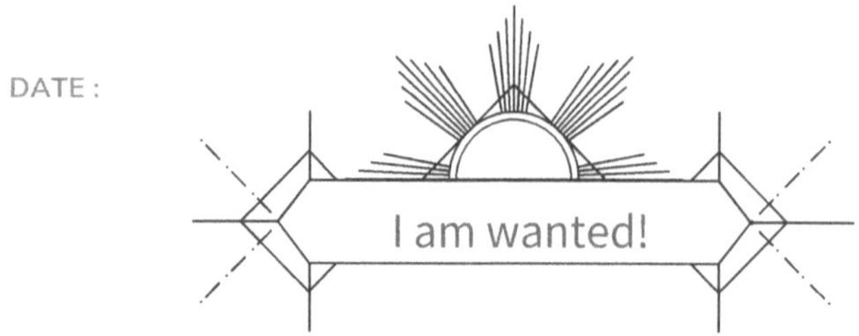

SELF-CARE REFLECTIONS

DATE :   M T W T F S S

DID I SET AN INTENTION FOR THE DAY? Y / N

TODAY'S ACCOMPLISHMENTS
BIG OR SMALL

1
2
3

BODY

CUPS OF WATER DRANK: _____
HOURS SLEPT LAST NIGHT: _____
MINUTES SPENT EXERCISING: _____
WHAT I ATE TODAY NOURISHED & ENERGIZED ME? Y / N

DIETARY NOTES: ____________
____
ONE WORD TO DESCRIBE HOW I FELT PHYSICALLY TODAY WAS _______________.

SOUL

DID I FEEL HOPEFUL TODAY? Y / N
MINUTES SPENT ON MEDITATIVE ACTIVITY OR IN A STATE OF FLOW: _____

ONE THING THAT GAVE ME PURPOSE TODAY WAS ______
____
____

SOMETHING I STRUGGLED WITH TODAY WAS ____________
____
____

MIND

WAS MY SELF-TALK TODAY KIND & COMPASSIONATE? Y / N

ONE THING I APPRECIATE ABOUT MYSELF IS _________________
____

SOMETHING I'M GRATEFUL FOR TODAY WAS _________________
____
____

DAILY DOODLE & Affirmation

DATE :

SELF-CARE REFLECTIONS

DATE :   M T W T F S S

DID I SET AN INTENTION FOR THE DAY? Y / N

TODAY'S ACCOMPLISHMENTS
BIG OR SMALL

1
2
3

BODY

CUPS OF WATER DRANK: _____
HOURS SLEPT LAST NIGHT: _____
MINUTES SPENT EXERCISING: _____
WHAT I ATE TODAY NOURISHED & ENERGIZED ME? Y / N

DIETARY NOTES: __________
____
ONE WORD TO DESCRIBE HOW I FELT PHYSICALLY TODAY WAS _____________.

SOUL

DID I FEEL HOPEFUL TODAY? Y / N
MINUTES SPENT ON MEDITATIVE ACTIVITY OR IN A STATE OF FLOW:

ONE THING THAT GAVE ME PURPOSE TODAY WAS ______
____
____

SOMETHING I STRUGGLED WITH TODAY WAS ___________
____
____

MIND

WAS MY SELF-TALK TODAY KIND & COMPASSIONATE? Y / N

ONE THING I APPRECIATE ABOUT MYSELF IS ______________________
____

SOMETHING I'M GRATEFUL FOR TODAY WAS _________________
____
____

DAILY DOODLE & AFFIRMATION

DATE :

SELF-CARE REFLECTIONS

DATE: M T W T F S S

DID I SET AN INTENTION FOR THE DAY? Y / N

TODAY'S ACCOMPLISHMENTS
BIG OR SMALL

1

2

3

BODY

CUPS OF WATER DRANK: _____
HOURS SLEPT LAST NIGHT: _____
MINUTES SPENT EXERCISING: _____
WHAT I ATE TODAY NOURISHED & ENERGIZED ME? Y / N

DIETARY NOTES: ____________
____
ONE WORD TO DESCRIBE HOW I FELT PHYSICALLY TODAY WAS _______________.

SOUL

DID I FEEL HOPEFUL TODAY? Y / N
MINUTES SPENT ON MEDITATIVE ACTIVITY OR IN A STATE OF FLOW: _____

ONE THING THAT GAVE ME PURPOSE TODAY WAS _______
____
____

SOMETHING I STRUGGLED WITH TODAY WAS ___________
____
____

MIND

WAS MY SELF-TALK TODAY KIND & COMPASSIONATE? Y / N

ONE THING I APPRECIATE ABOUT MYSELF IS ___________________
____

SOMETHING I'M GRATEFUL FOR TODAY WAS _________________
____
____

DAILY DOODLE & AFFIRMATION

DATE :

I am proud of myself!

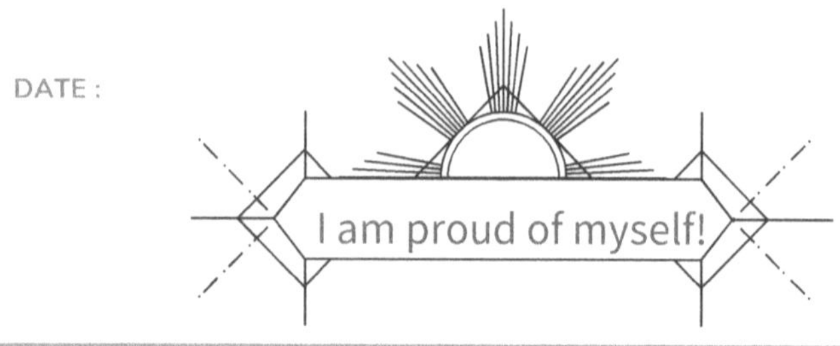

SELF-CARE REFLECTIONS

DATE: M T W T F S S

DID I SET AN INTENTION FOR THE DAY? Y / N

TODAY'S ACCOMPLISHMENTS
BIG OR SMALL

1 __________________________

2 __________________________

3 __________________________

BODY

CUPS OF WATER DRANK: _____

HOURS SLEPT LAST NIGHT: _____

MINUTES SPENT EXERCISING: _____

WHAT I ATE TODAY NOURISHED & ENERGIZED ME? Y / N

DIETARY NOTES: ____________

____

ONE WORD TO DESCRIBE HOW I FELT PHYSICALLY TODAY WAS __________.

SOUL

DID I FEEL HOPEFUL TODAY? Y / N

MINUTES SPENT ON MEDITATIVE ACTIVITY OR IN A STATE OF FLOW: _____

ONE THING THAT GAVE ME PURPOSE TODAY WAS _____

____

____

SOMETHING I STRUGGLED WITH TODAY WAS __________

____

____

MIND

WAS MY SELF-TALK TODAY KIND & COMPASSIONATE? Y / N

ONE THING I APPRECIATE ABOUT MYSELF IS ________________

____

SOMETHING I'M GRATEFUL FOR TODAY WAS ______________

____

____

DAILY DOODLE & Affirmation

DATE :

SELF-CARE REFLECTIONS

DATE :   M T W T F S S

DID I SET AN INTENTION FOR THE DAY? Y / N

TODAY'S ACCOMPLISHMENTS
BIG OR SMALL

1
2
3

BODY

CUPS OF WATER DRANK: _____
HOURS SLEPT LAST NIGHT: _____
MINUTES SPENT EXERCISING: _____
WHAT I ATE TODAY NOURISHED & ENERGIZED ME? Y / N

DIETARY NOTES: _____________
____
ONE WORD TO DESCRIBE HOW I FELT PHYSICALLY TODAY WAS _______________.

SOUL

DID I FEEL HOPEFUL TODAY? Y / N
MINUTES SPENT ON MEDITATIVE ACTIVITY OR IN A STATE OF FLOW: _____

ONE THING THAT GAVE ME PURPOSE TODAY WAS _______
____
____

SOMETHING I STRUGGLED WITH TODAY WAS ____________
____
____

MIND

WAS MY SELF-TALK TODAY KIND & COMPASSIONATE? Y / N

ONE THING I APPRECIATE ABOUT MYSELF IS ____________________
____

SOMETHING I'M GRATEFUL FOR TODAY WAS ________________
____
____

DAILY DOODLE & Affirmation

DATE :

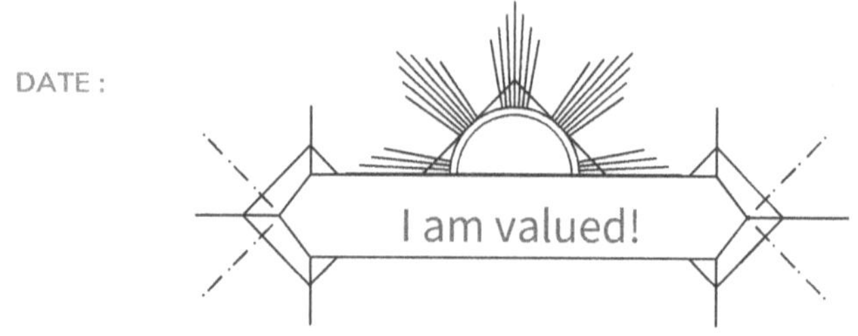

SELF-CARE REFLECTIONS

DATE: _______________________   M T W T F S S

DID I SET AN INTENTION FOR THE DAY? Y / N

TODAY'S ACCOMPLISHMENTS
BIG OR SMALL

1
2
3

BODY

CUPS OF WATER DRANK: _____
HOURS SLEPT LAST NIGHT: _____
MINUTES SPENT EXERCISING: _____
WHAT I ATE TODAY NOURISHED & ENERGIZED ME? Y / N

DIETARY NOTES: _____________
____
ONE WORD TO DESCRIBE HOW I FELT PHYSICALLY TODAY WAS _______________.

SOUL

DID I FEEL HOPEFUL TODAY? Y / N
MINUTES SPENT ON MEDITATIVE ACTIVITY OR IN A STATE OF FLOW: _____

ONE THING THAT GAVE ME PURPOSE TODAY WAS ______
____
____

SOMETHING I STRUGGLED WITH TODAY WAS ____________
____
____

MIND

WAS MY SELF-TALK TODAY KIND & COMPASSIONATE? Y / N

ONE THING I APPRECIATE ABOUT MYSELF IS ___________________
____

SOMETHING I'M GRATEFUL FOR TODAY WAS _______________
____
____

DAILY DOODLE & AFFIRMATION

DATE :

I am cool!

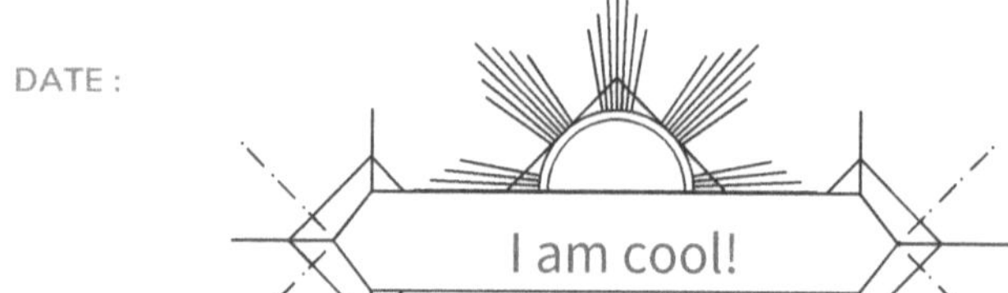

SELF-CARE REFLECTIONS

DATE :   M T W T F S S

DID I SET AN INTENTION FOR THE DAY? Y / N

TODAY'S ACCOMPLISHMENTS
BIG OR SMALL

1
2
3

BODY

CUPS OF WATER DRANK: _____
HOURS SLEPT LAST NIGHT: _____
MINUTES SPENT EXERCISING: _____
WHAT I ATE TODAY NOURISHED & ENERGIZED ME? Y / N

DIETARY NOTES: _____________
____
ONE WORD TO DESCRIBE HOW I FELT PHYSICALLY TODAY WAS _______________.

SOUL

DID I FEEL HOPEFUL TODAY? Y / N
MINUTES SPENT ON MEDITATIVE ACTIVITY OR IN A STATE OF FLOW: _____

ONE THING THAT GAVE ME PURPOSE TODAY WAS _______
____
____

SOMETHING I STRUGGLED WITH TODAY WAS ___________
____
____

MIND

WAS MY SELF-TALK TODAY KIND & COMPASSIONATE? Y / N

ONE THING I APPRECIATE ABOUT MYSELF IS _______________________
____

SOMETHING I'M GRATEFUL FOR TODAY WAS ________________
____
____

DAILY DOODLE & Affirmation

SELF-CARE REFLECTIONS

DATE: _______________________________   M T W T F S S

DID I SET AN INTENTION FOR THE DAY? Y / N

TODAY'S ACCOMPLISHMENTS
BIG OR SMALL

1 _______________________________

2 _______________________________

3 _______________________________

BODY

CUPS OF WATER DRANK: _____
HOURS SLEPT LAST NIGHT: _____
MINUTES SPENT EXERCISING: _____
WHAT I ATE TODAY NOURISHED &
ENERGIZED ME? Y / N

DIETARY NOTES: _____________
____
ONE WORD TO DESCRIBE
HOW I FELT PHYSICALLY
TODAY WAS _______________.

SOUL

DID I FEEL HOPEFUL
TODAY? Y / N
MINUTES SPENT ON
MEDITATIVE ACTIVITY OR
IN A STATE OF FLOW: _____

ONE THING THAT GAVE ME
PURPOSE TODAY WAS _______
____
____

SOMETHING I STRUGGLED
WITH TODAY WAS _____________
____
____

MIND

WAS MY SELF-TALK TODAY KIND
& COMPASSIONATE? Y / N

ONE THING I APPRECIATE ABOUT
MYSELF IS _______________________
____

SOMETHING I'M GRATEFUL FOR
TODAY WAS _____________________
____
____

DAILY DOODLE & AFFIRMATION

DATE :

I am brilliant!

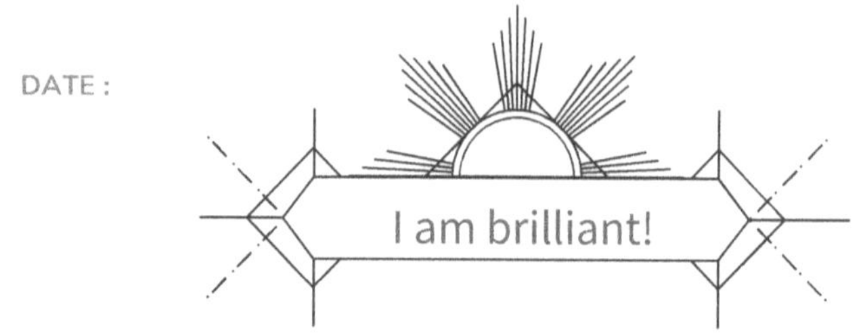

SELF-CARE REFLECTIONS

DATE: _______________   M T W T F S S

DID I SET AN INTENTION FOR THE DAY? Y / N

____

____

____

TODAY'S ACCOMPLISHMENTS
BIG OR SMALL

1 _____________________________________

2 _____________________________________

3 _____________________________________

BODY

CUPS OF WATER DRANK: _____

HOURS SLEPT LAST NIGHT: _____

MINUTES SPENT EXERCISING: _____

WHAT I ATE TODAY NOURISHED & ENERGIZED ME? Y / N

DIETARY NOTES: _______________

____

ONE WORD TO DESCRIBE HOW I FELT PHYSICALLY TODAY WAS _______________.

SOUL

DID I FEEL HOPEFUL TODAY? Y / N

MINUTES SPENT ON MEDITATIVE ACTIVITY OR IN A STATE OF FLOW: _____

ONE THING THAT GAVE ME PURPOSE TODAY WAS _____

____

____

SOMETHING I STRUGGLED WITH TODAY WAS _______________

____

____

MIND

WAS MY SELF-TALK TODAY KIND & COMPASSIONATE? Y / N

ONE THING I APPRECIATE ABOUT MYSELF IS _______________

____

SOMETHING I'M GRATEFUL FOR TODAY WAS _______________

____

____

DAILY DOODLE & AFFIRMATION

DATE :

SELF-CARE REFLECTIONS

DATE :   M T W T F S S

DID I SET AN INTENTION FOR THE DAY? Y / N

TODAY'S ACCOMPLISHMENTS
BIG OR SMALL

1

2

3

BODY

CUPS OF WATER DRANK: _____
HOURS SLEPT LAST NIGHT: _____
MINUTES SPENT EXERCISING: _____
WHAT I ATE TODAY NOURISHED & ENERGIZED ME? Y / N

DIETARY NOTES: ______________
____
ONE WORD TO DESCRIBE HOW I FELT PHYSICALLY TODAY WAS ____________.

SOUL

DID I FEEL HOPEFUL TODAY? Y / N
MINUTES SPENT ON MEDITATIVE ACTIVITY OR IN A STATE OF FLOW: _____

ONE THING THAT GAVE ME PURPOSE TODAY WAS ______
____
____

SOMETHING I STRUGGLED WITH TODAY WAS ____________
____
____

MIND

WAS MY SELF-TALK TODAY KIND & COMPASSIONATE? Y / N

ONE THING I APPRECIATE ABOUT MYSELF IS ___________________
____

SOMETHING I'M GRATEFUL FOR TODAY WAS ________________
____
____

DAILY DOODLE & Affirmation

DATE :

SELF-CARE REFLECTIONS

DATE: M T W T F S S

DID I SET AN INTENTION FOR THE DAY? Y / N

TODAY'S ACCOMPLISHMENTS
BIG OR SMALL

1
2
3

BODY

CUPS OF WATER DRANK: _____
HOURS SLEPT LAST NIGHT: _____
MINUTES SPENT EXERCISING: _____
WHAT I ATE TODAY NOURISHED &
ENERGIZED ME? Y / N

DIETARY NOTES: ___________
____
ONE WORD TO DESCRIBE
HOW I FELT PHYSICALLY
TODAY WAS ______________.

SOUL

DID I FEEL HOPEFUL
TODAY? Y / N
MINUTES SPENT ON
MEDITATIVE ACTIVITY OR
IN A STATE OF FLOW: _____

ONE THING THAT GAVE ME
PURPOSE TODAY WAS _____
____
____

SOMETHING I STRUGGLED
WITH TODAY WAS ___________
____
____

MIND

WAS MY SELF-TALK TODAY KIND
& COMPASSIONATE? Y / N

ONE THING I APPRECIATE ABOUT
MYSELF IS ___________________
____

SOMETHING I'M GRATEFUL FOR
TODAY WAS ___________________
____
____

DAILY DOODLE & AFFIRMATION

DATE :

I make it happen!

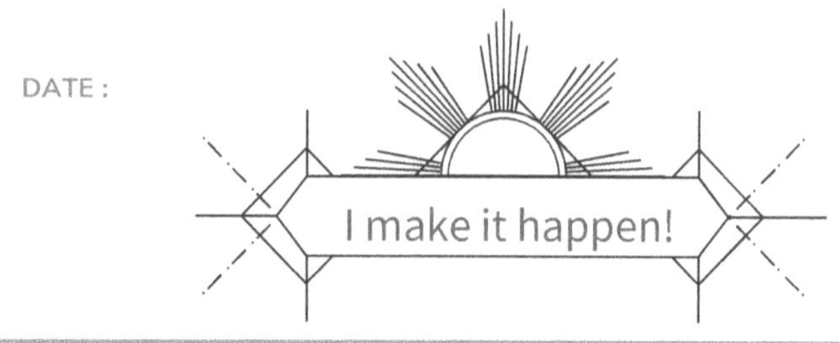

SELF-CARE REFLECTIONS

DATE: _______________   M T W T F S S

DID I SET AN INTENTION FOR THE DAY? Y / N

____

____

____

TODAY'S ACCOMPLISHMENTS
BIG OR SMALL

1 ______________________________

2 ______________________________

3 ______________________________

BODY

CUPS OF WATER DRANK: ______

HOURS SLEPT LAST NIGHT: ______

MINUTES SPENT EXERCISING: ______

WHAT I ATE TODAY NOURISHED & ENERGIZED ME? Y / N

DIETARY NOTES: ______________

____

ONE WORD TO DESCRIBE HOW I FELT PHYSICALLY TODAY WAS ______________.

SOUL

DID I FEEL HOPEFUL TODAY? Y / N

MINUTES SPENT ON MEDITATIVE ACTIVITY OR IN A STATE OF FLOW: ______

ONE THING THAT GAVE ME PURPOSE TODAY WAS ______

____

____

SOMETHING I STRUGGLED WITH TODAY WAS ___________

____

____

MIND

WAS MY SELF-TALK TODAY KIND & COMPASSIONATE? Y / N

ONE THING I APPRECIATE ABOUT MYSELF IS ___________________

____

SOMETHING I'M GRATEFUL FOR TODAY WAS ________________

____

____

DAILY DOODLE & AFFIRMATION

SELF-CARE REFLECTIONS

DATE :   M T W T F S S

DID I SET AN INTENTION FOR THE DAY? Y / N

TODAY'S ACCOMPLISHMENTS
BIG OR SMALL

1
2
3

BODY

CUPS OF WATER DRANK: _____
HOURS SLEPT LAST NIGHT: _____
MINUTES SPENT EXERCISING: _____
WHAT I ATE TODAY NOURISHED &
ENERGIZED ME? Y / N

DIETARY NOTES: ______________
____
ONE WORD TO DESCRIBE
HOW I FELT PHYSICALLY
TODAY WAS _________________.

SOUL

DID I FEEL HOPEFUL
TODAY? Y / N
MINUTES SPENT ON
MEDITATIVE ACTIVITY OR
IN A STATE OF FLOW:

ONE THING THAT GAVE ME
PURPOSE TODAY WAS ______

____
____

SOMETHING I STRUGGLED
WITH TODAY WAS ____________

____
____

MIND

WAS MY SELF-TALK TODAY KIND
& COMPASSIONATE? Y / N

ONE THING I APPRECIATE ABOUT
MYSELF IS ______________________

____

SOMETHING I'M GRATEFUL FOR
TODAY WAS __________________

____
____

DAILY DOODLE & Affirmation

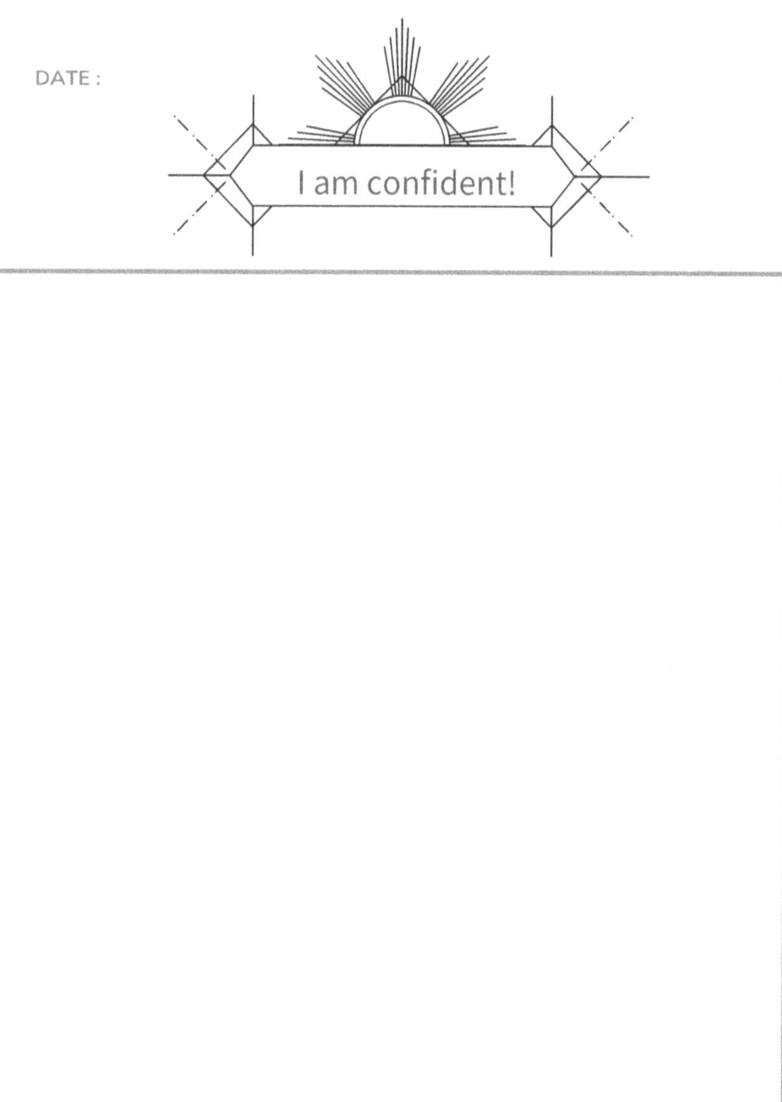

SELF-CARE REFLECTIONS

DATE :   M T W T F S S

DID I SET AN INTENTION FOR THE DAY? Y / N

TODAY'S ACCOMPLISHMENTS
BIG OR SMALL

1
2
3

BODY

CUPS OF WATER DRANK: _____
HOURS SLEPT LAST NIGHT: _____
MINUTES SPENT EXERCISING: _____
WHAT I ATE TODAY NOURISHED &
ENERGIZED ME? Y / N

DIETARY NOTES: _____________
____
ONE WORD TO DESCRIBE
HOW I FELT PHYSICALLY
TODAY WAS _______________.

SOUL

DID I FEEL HOPEFUL
TODAY? Y / N
MINUTES SPENT ON
MEDITATIVE ACTIVITY OR
IN A STATE OF FLOW: _____

ONE THING THAT GAVE ME
PURPOSE TODAY WAS _______
____
____

SOMETHING I STRUGGLED
WITH TODAY WAS ____________
____
____

MIND

WAS MY SELF-TALK TODAY KIND
& COMPASSIONATE? Y / N

ONE THING I APPRECIATE ABOUT
MYSELF IS ____________________
____

SOMETHING I'M GRATEFUL FOR
TODAY WAS _________________
____
____

DAILY DOODLE & Affirmation

DATE :

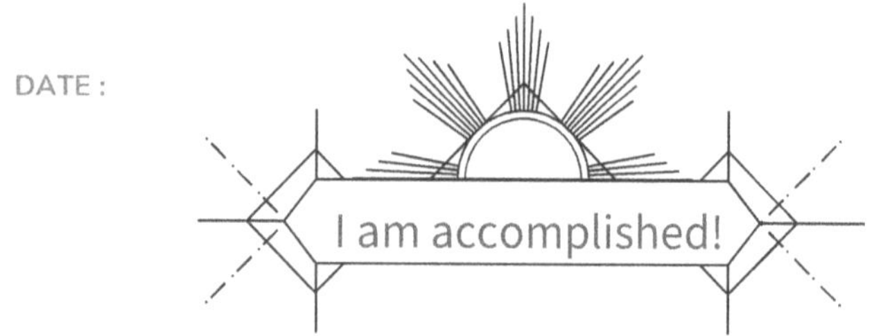

SELF-CARE REFLECTIONS

DATE :   M T W T F S S

DID I SET AN INTENTION FOR THE DAY? Y / N

TODAY'S ACCOMPLISHMENTS
BIG OR SMALL

1

2

3

BODY

CUPS OF WATER DRANK: _____
HOURS SLEPT LAST NIGHT: _____
MINUTES SPENT EXERCISING: _____
WHAT I ATE TODAY NOURISHED & ENERGIZED ME? Y / N

DIETARY NOTES: ___________
____
ONE WORD TO DESCRIBE HOW I FELT PHYSICALLY TODAY WAS _______________.

SOUL

DID I FEEL HOPEFUL TODAY? Y / N
MINUTES SPENT ON MEDITATIVE ACTIVITY OR IN A STATE OF FLOW: _____

ONE THING THAT GAVE ME PURPOSE TODAY WAS ______
____
____

SOMETHING I STRUGGLED WITH TODAY WAS ___________
____
____

MIND

WAS MY SELF-TALK TODAY KIND & COMPASSIONATE? Y / N

ONE THING I APPRECIATE ABOUT MYSELF IS ___________________
____

SOMETHING I'M GRATEFUL FOR TODAY WAS _______________
____
____

DAILY DOODLE & AFFIRMATION

DATE :

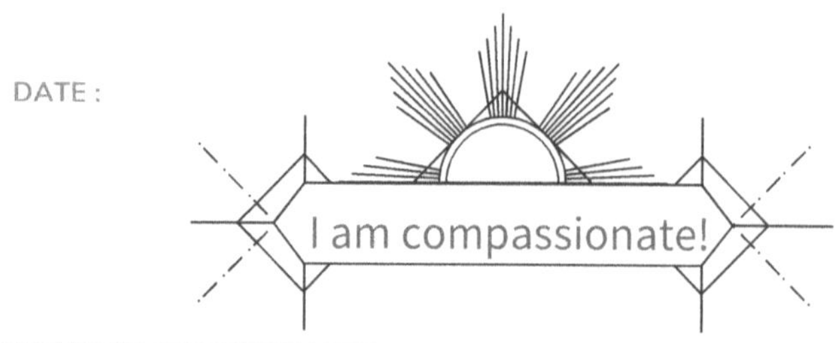

SELF-CARE REFLECTIONS

DATE :   M T W T F S S

DID I SET AN INTENTION FOR THE DAY? Y / N

TODAY'S ACCOMPLISHMENTS
BIG OR SMALL

1 ____________________

2 ____________________

3 ____________________

BODY

CUPS OF WATER DRANK: _____

HOURS SLEPT LAST NIGHT: _____

MINUTES SPENT EXERCISING: _____

WHAT I ATE TODAY NOURISHED & ENERGIZED ME? Y / N

DIETARY NOTES: _____________

____

ONE WORD TO DESCRIBE HOW I FELT PHYSICALLY TODAY WAS ________________.

SOUL

DID I FEEL HOPEFUL TODAY? Y / N

MINUTES SPENT ON MEDITATIVE ACTIVITY OR IN A STATE OF FLOW: _____

ONE THING THAT GAVE ME PURPOSE TODAY WAS ______

____

____

SOMETHING I STRUGGLED WITH TODAY WAS ____________

____

____

MIND

WAS MY SELF-TALK TODAY KIND & COMPASSIONATE? Y / N

ONE THING I APPRECIATE ABOUT MYSELF IS ____________________

____

SOMETHING I'M GRATEFUL FOR TODAY WAS __________________

____

____

DAILY DOODLE & Affirmation

SELF-CARE REFLECTIONS

DATE :   M T W T F S S

DID I SET AN INTENTION FOR THE DAY? Y / N

TODAY'S ACCOMPLISHMENTS
BIG OR SMALL

1

2

3

BODY

CUPS OF WATER DRANK: _____
HOURS SLEPT LAST NIGHT: _____
MINUTES SPENT EXERCISING: _____
WHAT I ATE TODAY NOURISHED & ENERGIZED ME? Y / N

DIETARY NOTES: ___________
____
ONE WORD TO DESCRIBE HOW I FELT PHYSICALLY TODAY WAS ______________.

SOUL

DID I FEEL HOPEFUL TODAY? Y / N
MINUTES SPENT ON MEDITATIVE ACTIVITY OR IN A STATE OF FLOW: _____

ONE THING THAT GAVE ME PURPOSE TODAY WAS ______
____
____

SOMETHING I STRUGGLED WITH TODAY WAS ___________
____
____

MIND

WAS MY SELF-TALK TODAY KIND & COMPASSIONATE? Y / N

ONE THING I APPRECIATE ABOUT MYSELF IS ___________________
____

SOMETHING I'M GRATEFUL FOR TODAY WAS ________________
____
____

DAILY DOODLE & Affirmation

DATE :

SELF-CARE REFLECTIONS

DATE :   M T W T F S S

DID I SET AN INTENTION FOR THE DAY? Y / N

TODAY'S ACCOMPLISHMENTS
BIG OR SMALL

1
2
3

BODY

CUPS OF WATER DRANK: ____
HOURS SLEPT LAST NIGHT: ____
MINUTES SPENT EXERCISING: ____
WHAT I ATE TODAY NOURISHED &
ENERGIZED ME? Y / N

DIETARY NOTES: ____________
____
ONE WORD TO DESCRIBE
HOW I FELT PHYSICALLY
TODAY WAS ______________.

SOUL

DID I FEEL HOPEFUL
TODAY? Y / N
MINUTES SPENT ON
MEDITATIVE ACTIVITY OR
IN A STATE OF FLOW: ____

ONE THING THAT GAVE ME
PURPOSE TODAY WAS ______
____
____

SOMETHING I STRUGGLED
WITH TODAY WAS ____________
____
____

MIND

WAS MY SELF-TALK TODAY KIND
& COMPASSIONATE? Y / N

ONE THING I APPRECIATE ABOUT
MYSELF IS ____________________
____

SOMETHING I'M GRATEFUL FOR
TODAY WAS ____________________
____
____

DAILY DOODLE & AFFIRMATION

DATE :

I am grateful!

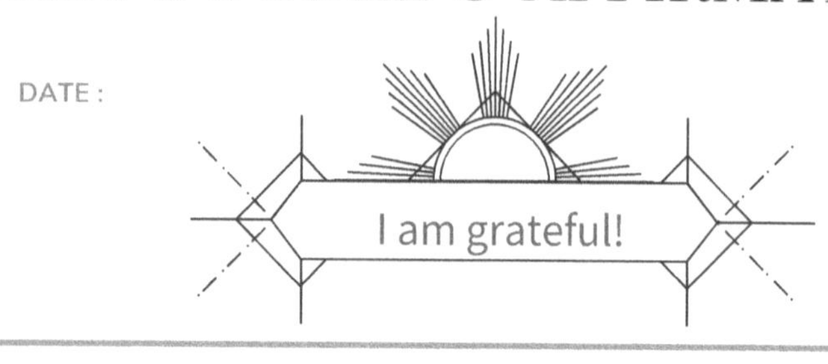

SELF-CARE REFLECTIONS

DATE :   M T W T F S S

DID I SET AN INTENTION FOR THE DAY? Y / N

TODAY'S ACCOMPLISHMENTS
BIG OR SMALL

1

2

3

BODY

CUPS OF WATER DRANK: _____

HOURS SLEPT LAST NIGHT: _____

MINUTES SPENT EXERCISING: _____

WHAT I ATE TODAY NOURISHED & ENERGIZED ME? Y / N

DIETARY NOTES: _____________

____

ONE WORD TO DESCRIBE HOW I FELT PHYSICALLY TODAY WAS _____________.

SOUL

DID I FEEL HOPEFUL TODAY? Y / N

MINUTES SPENT ON MEDITATIVE ACTIVITY OR IN A STATE OF FLOW: _____

ONE THING THAT GAVE ME PURPOSE TODAY WAS _____

____

____

SOMETHING I STRUGGLED WITH TODAY WAS _____________

____

____

MIND

WAS MY SELF-TALK TODAY KIND & COMPASSIONATE? Y / N

ONE THING I APPRECIATE ABOUT MYSELF IS _____________

____

SOMETHING I'M GRATEFUL FOR TODAY WAS _____________

____

____

DAILY DOODLE & Affirmation

SELF-CARE REFLECTIONS

DATE: M T W T F S S

DID I SET AN INTENTION FOR THE DAY? Y / N

TODAY'S ACCOMPLISHMENTS

BIG OR SMALL

1

2

3

BODY

CUPS OF WATER DRANK: _____

HOURS SLEPT LAST NIGHT: _____

MINUTES SPENT EXERCISING: _____

WHAT I ATE TODAY NOURISHED & ENERGIZED ME? Y / N

DIETARY NOTES: _____________

____

ONE WORD TO DESCRIBE HOW I FELT PHYSICALLY TODAY WAS _______________.

SOUL

DID I FEEL HOPEFUL TODAY? Y / N

MINUTES SPENT ON MEDITATIVE ACTIVITY OR IN A STATE OF FLOW: _____

ONE THING THAT GAVE ME PURPOSE TODAY WAS _____

____

____

SOMETHING I STRUGGLED WITH TODAY WAS ___________

____

____

MIND

WAS MY SELF-TALK TODAY KIND & COMPASSIONATE? Y / N

ONE THING I APPRECIATE ABOUT MYSELF IS _______________

____

SOMETHING I'M GRATEFUL FOR TODAY WAS _______________

____

____

DAILY DOODLE & AFFIRMATION

DATE :

SELF-CARE REFLECTIONS

DATE :   M T W T F S S

DID I SET AN INTENTION FOR THE DAY? Y / N	**TODAY'S ACCOMPLISHMENTS** BIG OR SMALL

1 ________
2 ________
3 ________

BODY

CUPS OF WATER DRANK: _____
HOURS SLEPT LAST NIGHT: _____
MINUTES SPENT EXERCISING: _____
WHAT I ATE TODAY NOURISHED & ENERGIZED ME? Y / N

DIETARY NOTES: _____________
____
ONE WORD TO DESCRIBE HOW I FELT PHYSICALLY TODAY WAS _______________.

SOUL

DID I FEEL HOPEFUL TODAY? Y / N
MINUTES SPENT ON MEDITATIVE ACTIVITY OR IN A STATE OF FLOW: _____

ONE THING THAT GAVE ME PURPOSE TODAY WAS _______
____
____

SOMETHING I STRUGGLED WITH TODAY WAS _____________
____
____

MIND

WAS MY SELF-TALK TODAY KIND & COMPASSIONATE? Y / N

ONE THING I APPRECIATE ABOUT MYSELF IS ___________________
____

SOMETHING I'M GRATEFUL FOR TODAY WAS _________________
____
____

DAILY DOODLE & Affirmation

DATE :

SELF-CARE REFLECTIONS

DATE :   M T W T F S S

DID I SET AN INTENTION FOR THE DAY? Y / N

TODAY'S ACCOMPLISHMENTS
BIG OR SMALL

1

2

3

BODY

CUPS OF WATER DRANK: _____
HOURS SLEPT LAST NIGHT: _____
MINUTES SPENT EXERCISING: _____
WHAT I ATE TODAY NOURISHED & ENERGIZED ME? Y / N

DIETARY NOTES: _____________
____
ONE WORD TO DESCRIBE HOW I FELT PHYSICALLY TODAY WAS _____________.

SOUL

DID I FEEL HOPEFUL TODAY? Y / N
MINUTES SPENT ON MEDITATIVE ACTIVITY OR IN A STATE OF FLOW: _____

ONE THING THAT GAVE ME PURPOSE TODAY WAS _____
____
____

SOMETHING I STRUGGLED WITH TODAY WAS ___________
____
____

MIND

WAS MY SELF-TALK TODAY KIND & COMPASSIONATE? Y / N

ONE THING I APPRECIATE ABOUT MYSELF IS _______________
____

SOMETHING I'M GRATEFUL FOR TODAY WAS _______________
____
____

DAILY DOODLE & AFFIRMATION

DATE :

SELF-CARE REFLECTIONS

DATE :   M T W T F S S

DID I SET AN INTENTION FOR THE DAY? Y / N

TODAY'S ACCOMPLISHMENTS

BIG OR SMALL

1

2

3

BODY

CUPS OF WATER DRANK: _____
HOURS SLEPT LAST NIGHT: _____
MINUTES SPENT EXERCISING: _____
WHAT I ATE TODAY NOURISHED & ENERGIZED ME? Y / N

DIETARY NOTES: ___________
____
ONE WORD TO DESCRIBE HOW I FELT PHYSICALLY TODAY WAS ____________.

SOUL

DID I FEEL HOPEFUL TODAY? Y / N
MINUTES SPENT ON MEDITATIVE ACTIVITY OR IN A STATE OF FLOW: _____

ONE THING THAT GAVE ME PURPOSE TODAY WAS _____
____
____

SOMETHING I STRUGGLED WITH TODAY WAS ___________
____
____

MIND

WAS MY SELF-TALK TODAY KIND & COMPASSIONATE? Y / N

ONE THING I APPRECIATE ABOUT MYSELF IS ______________
____

SOMETHING I'M GRATEFUL FOR TODAY WAS ______________
____
____

DAILY DOODLE & AFFIRMATION

DATE :

I love my body!

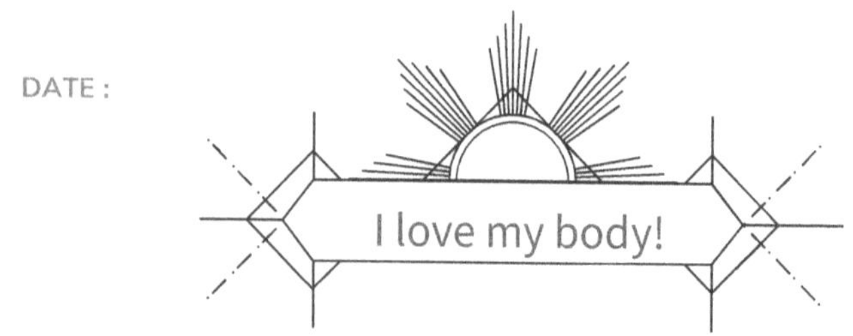

SELF-CARE REFLECTIONS

DATE: M T W T F S S

DID I SET AN INTENTION FOR THE DAY? Y / N

TODAY'S ACCOMPLISHMENTS
BIG OR SMALL

1

2

3

BODY

CUPS OF WATER DRANK: _____
HOURS SLEPT LAST NIGHT: _____
MINUTES SPENT EXERCISING: _____
WHAT I ATE TODAY NOURISHED & ENERGIZED ME? Y / N

DIETARY NOTES: ______________

____

ONE WORD TO DESCRIBE HOW I FELT PHYSICALLY TODAY WAS ______________.

SOUL

DID I FEEL HOPEFUL TODAY? Y / N
MINUTES SPENT ON MEDITATIVE ACTIVITY OR IN A STATE OF FLOW: _____

ONE THING THAT GAVE ME PURPOSE TODAY WAS _____

____

____

SOMETHING I STRUGGLED WITH TODAY WAS ______________

____

____

MIND

WAS MY SELF-TALK TODAY KIND & COMPASSIONATE? Y / N

ONE THING I APPRECIATE ABOUT MYSELF IS ______________

____

SOMETHING I'M GRATEFUL FOR TODAY WAS ______________

____

____

DAILY DOODLE & Affirmation

DATE :

SELF-CARE REFLECTIONS

DATE: ________________________   M T W T F S S

DID I SET AN INTENTION FOR THE DAY? Y / N

TODAY'S ACCOMPLISHMENTS
BIG OR SMALL

1
2
3

BODY

CUPS OF WATER DRANK: _____
HOURS SLEPT LAST NIGHT: _____
MINUTES SPENT EXERCISING: _____
WHAT I ATE TODAY NOURISHED & ENERGIZED ME? Y / N

DIETARY NOTES: ____________
____
ONE WORD TO DESCRIBE HOW I FELT PHYSICALLY TODAY WAS _____________.

SOUL

DID I FEEL HOPEFUL TODAY? Y / N
MINUTES SPENT ON MEDITATIVE ACTIVITY OR IN A STATE OF FLOW: _____

ONE THING THAT GAVE ME PURPOSE TODAY WAS ______
____
____

SOMETHING I STRUGGLED WITH TODAY WAS ___________
____
____

MIND

WAS MY SELF-TALK TODAY KIND & COMPASSIONATE? Y / N

ONE THING I APPRECIATE ABOUT MYSELF IS ________________
____

SOMETHING I'M GRATEFUL FOR TODAY WAS ________________
____
____

DAILY DOODLE & Affirmation

SELF-CARE REFLECTIONS

DATE: M T W T F S S

DID I SET AN INTENTION FOR THE DAY? Y / N

TODAY'S ACCOMPLISHMENTS
BIG OR SMALL

1
2
3

BODY

CUPS OF WATER DRANK: _____
HOURS SLEPT LAST NIGHT: _____
MINUTES SPENT EXERCISING: _____
WHAT I ATE TODAY NOURISHED &
ENERGIZED ME? Y / N

DIETARY NOTES: ____________
____
ONE WORD TO DESCRIBE
HOW I FELT PHYSICALLY
TODAY WAS ______________.

SOUL

DID I FEEL HOPEFUL
TODAY? Y / N
MINUTES SPENT ON
MEDITATIVE ACTIVITY OR
IN A STATE OF FLOW: _____

ONE THING THAT GAVE ME
PURPOSE TODAY WAS _____
____
____

SOMETHING I STRUGGLED
WITH TODAY WAS ___________
____
____

MIND

WAS MY SELF-TALK TODAY KIND
& COMPASSIONATE? Y / N

ONE THING I APPRECIATE ABOUT
MYSELF IS ___________________
____

SOMETHING I'M GRATEFUL FOR
TODAY WAS ________________
____
____

DAILY DOODLE & AFFIRMATION

DATE :

I am always growing!

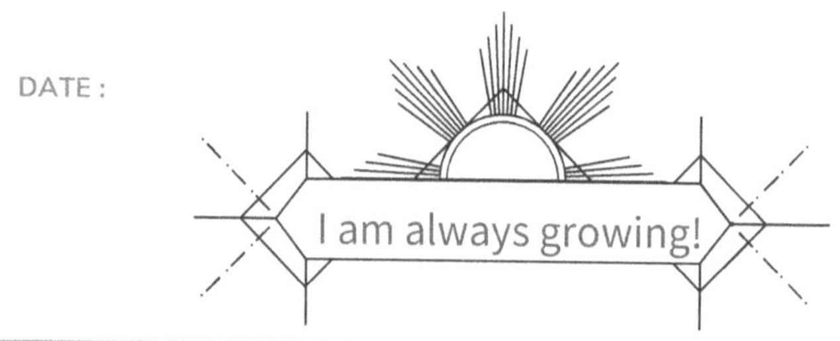

SELF-CARE REFLECTIONS

DATE :   M T W T F S S

DID I SET AN INTENTION FOR THE DAY? Y / N

TODAY'S ACCOMPLISHMENTS
BIG OR SMALL

1

2

3

BODY

CUPS OF WATER DRANK: _____
HOURS SLEPT LAST NIGHT: _____
MINUTES SPENT EXERCISING: _____
WHAT I ATE TODAY NOURISHED &
ENERGIZED ME? Y / N

DIETARY NOTES: ______________
____
ONE WORD TO DESCRIBE
HOW I FELT PHYSICALLY
TODAY WAS ________________.

SOUL

DID I FEEL HOPEFUL
TODAY? Y / N
MINUTES SPENT ON
MEDITATIVE ACTIVITY OR
IN A STATE OF FLOW: _____

ONE THING THAT GAVE ME
PURPOSE TODAY WAS _______
____
____

SOMETHING I STRUGGLED
WITH TODAY WAS ____________
____
____

MIND

WAS MY SELF-TALK TODAY KIND
& COMPASSIONATE? Y / N

ONE THING I APPRECIATE ABOUT
MYSELF IS ____________________
____

SOMETHING I'M GRATEFUL FOR
TODAY WAS ___________________
____
____

DAILY DOODLE & AFFIRMATION

DATE :

SELF-CARE REFLECTIONS

DATE: _______________   M T W T F S S

DID I SET AN INTENTION FOR THE DAY? Y / N

TODAY'S ACCOMPLISHMENTS
BIG OR SMALL

1 ______________________________
2 ______________________________
3 ______________________________

BODY

CUPS OF WATER DRANK: _____
HOURS SLEPT LAST NIGHT: _____
MINUTES SPENT EXERCISING: _____
WHAT I ATE TODAY NOURISHED & ENERGIZED ME? Y / N

DIETARY NOTES: ______________
____
ONE WORD TO DESCRIBE HOW I FELT PHYSICALLY TODAY WAS ______________.

SOUL

DID I FEEL HOPEFUL TODAY? Y / N
MINUTES SPENT ON MEDITATIVE ACTIVITY OR IN A STATE OF FLOW: _____

ONE THING THAT GAVE ME PURPOSE TODAY WAS _____
____
____

SOMETHING I STRUGGLED WITH TODAY WAS ______________
____
____

MIND

WAS MY SELF-TALK TODAY KIND & COMPASSIONATE? Y / N

ONE THING I APPRECIATE ABOUT MYSELF IS ______________
____

SOMETHING I'M GRATEFUL FOR TODAY WAS ______________
____
____

DAILY DOODLE & AFFIRMATION

DATE :

I am radiant!

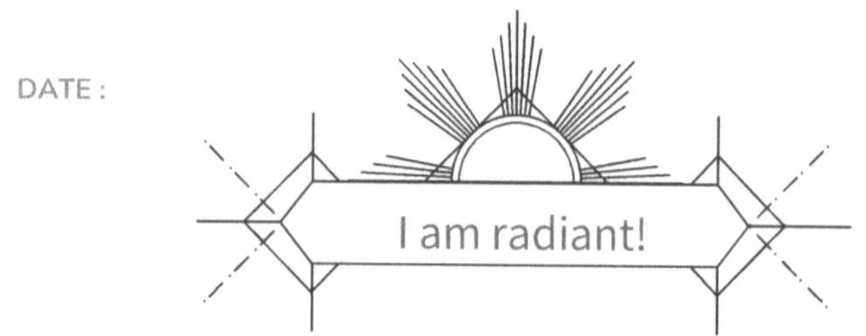

SELF-CARE REFLECTIONS

DATE: M T W T F S S

DID I SET AN INTENTION FOR THE DAY? Y / N

TODAY'S ACCOMPLISHMENTS
BIG OR SMALL

1

2

3

BODY

CUPS OF WATER DRANK: _____
HOURS SLEPT LAST NIGHT: _____
MINUTES SPENT EXERCISING: _____
WHAT I ATE TODAY NOURISHED & ENERGIZED ME? Y / N

DIETARY NOTES: _____________
____
ONE WORD TO DESCRIBE HOW I FELT PHYSICALLY TODAY WAS _____________.

SOUL

DID I FEEL HOPEFUL TODAY? Y / N
MINUTES SPENT ON MEDITATIVE ACTIVITY OR IN A STATE OF FLOW: _____

ONE THING THAT GAVE ME PURPOSE TODAY WAS _____
____
____

SOMETHING I STRUGGLED WITH TODAY WAS _____________
____
____

MIND

WAS MY SELF-TALK TODAY KIND & COMPASSIONATE? Y / N

ONE THING I APPRECIATE ABOUT MYSELF IS _______________
____

SOMETHING I'M GRATEFUL FOR TODAY WAS _______________
____
____

DAILY DOODLE & AFFIRMATION

DATE :

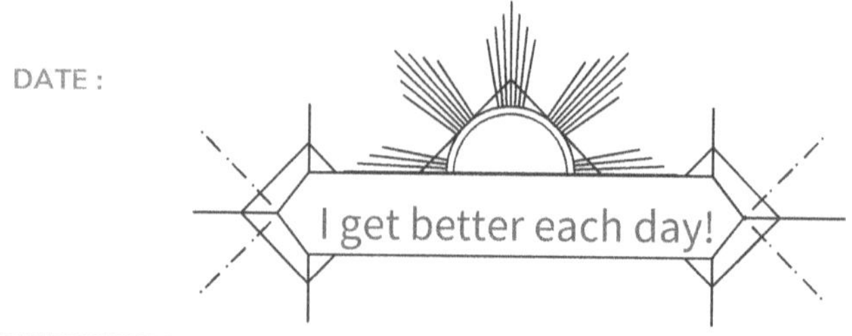

SELF-CARE REFLECTIONS

DATE: ___________   M T W T F S S

DID I SET AN INTENTION FOR THE DAY? Y / N

____

____

____

TODAY'S ACCOMPLISHMENTS
BIG OR SMALL

1 ________________________________

2 ________________________________

3 ________________________________

BODY

CUPS OF WATER DRANK: ______
HOURS SLEPT LAST NIGHT: ______
MINUTES SPENT EXERCISING: ______
WHAT I ATE TODAY NOURISHED & ENERGIZED ME? Y / N

DIETARY NOTES: ____________

____

ONE WORD TO DESCRIBE HOW I FELT PHYSICALLY TODAY WAS ____________.

SOUL

DID I FEEL HOPEFUL TODAY? Y / N
MINUTES SPENT ON MEDITATIVE ACTIVITY OR IN A STATE OF FLOW: ______

ONE THING THAT GAVE ME PURPOSE TODAY WAS ______

____

____

SOMETHING I STRUGGLED WITH TODAY WAS ____________

____

____

MIND

WAS MY SELF-TALK TODAY KIND & COMPASSIONATE? Y / N

ONE THING I APPRECIATE ABOUT MYSELF IS ____________

____

SOMETHING I'M GRATEFUL FOR TODAY WAS ____________

____

____

DATE :

SELF-CARE REFLECTIONS

DATE: ______________________   M T W T F S S

DID I SET AN INTENTION FOR THE DAY? Y / N

TODAY'S ACCOMPLISHMENTS
BIG OR SMALL

1

2

3

BODY

CUPS OF WATER DRANK: _____
HOURS SLEPT LAST NIGHT: _____
MINUTES SPENT EXERCISING: _____
WHAT I ATE TODAY NOURISHED & ENERGIZED ME? Y / N

DIETARY NOTES: ______________
____
ONE WORD TO DESCRIBE HOW I FELT PHYSICALLY TODAY WAS _______________.

SOUL

DID I FEEL HOPEFUL TODAY? Y / N
MINUTES SPENT ON MEDITATIVE ACTIVITY OR IN A STATE OF FLOW: _____

ONE THING THAT GAVE ME PURPOSE TODAY WAS _____
____
____

SOMETHING I STRUGGLED WITH TODAY WAS ____________
____
____

MIND

WAS MY SELF-TALK TODAY KIND & COMPASSIONATE? Y / N

ONE THING I APPRECIATE ABOUT MYSELF IS _______________________
____

SOMETHING I'M GRATEFUL FOR TODAY WAS ___________________
____
____

DAILY DOODLE & AFFIRMATION

DATE :

I deserve good!

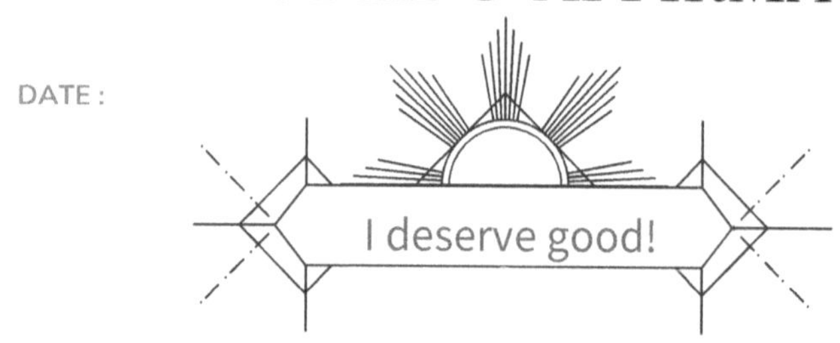

SELF-CARE REFLECTIONS

DATE : M T W T F S S

DID I SET AN INTENTION FOR THE DAY? Y / N

TODAY'S ACCOMPLISHMENTS
BIG OR SMALL

1
2
3

BODY

CUPS OF WATER DRANK: _____
HOURS SLEPT LAST NIGHT: _____
MINUTES SPENT EXERCISING: _____
WHAT I ATE TODAY NOURISHED & ENERGIZED ME? Y / N

DIETARY NOTES: ____________
____
ONE WORD TO DESCRIBE HOW I FELT PHYSICALLY TODAY WAS ______________.

SOUL

DID I FEEL HOPEFUL TODAY? Y / N
MINUTES SPENT ON MEDITATIVE ACTIVITY OR IN A STATE OF FLOW: _____

ONE THING THAT GAVE ME PURPOSE TODAY WAS ______
____
____

SOMETHING I STRUGGLED WITH TODAY WAS ____________
____
____

MIND

WAS MY SELF-TALK TODAY KIND & COMPASSIONATE? Y / N

ONE THING I APPRECIATE ABOUT MYSELF IS ______________________
____

SOMETHING I'M GRATEFUL FOR TODAY WAS ________________
____
____

DAILY DOODLE & AFFIRMATION

DATE :

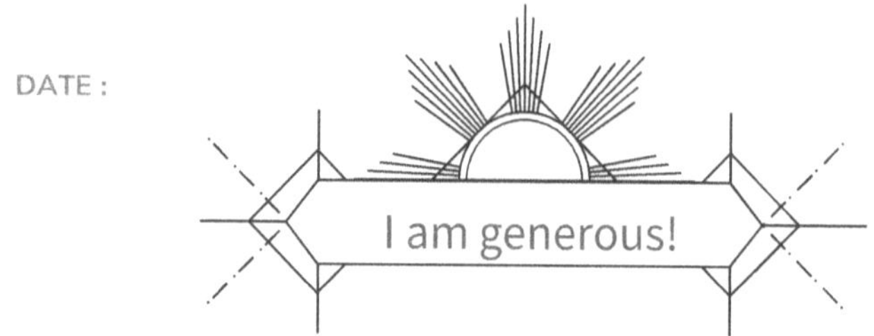

SELF-CARE REFLECTIONS

DATE :   M T W T F S S

DID I SET AN INTENTION FOR THE DAY? Y / N

TODAY'S ACCOMPLISHMENTS
BIG OR SMALL

1
2
3

BODY

CUPS OF WATER DRANK: _____
HOURS SLEPT LAST NIGHT: _____
MINUTES SPENT EXERCISING: _____
WHAT I ATE TODAY NOURISHED & ENERGIZED ME? Y / N

DIETARY NOTES: _____________
____
ONE WORD TO DESCRIBE HOW I FELT PHYSICALLY TODAY WAS _____________.

SOUL

DID I FEEL HOPEFUL TODAY? Y / N
MINUTES SPENT ON MEDITATIVE ACTIVITY OR IN A STATE OF FLOW:

ONE THING THAT GAVE ME PURPOSE TODAY WAS _____
____
____

SOMETHING I STRUGGLED WITH TODAY WAS ___________
____
____

MIND

WAS MY SELF-TALK TODAY KIND & COMPASSIONATE? Y / N

ONE THING I APPRECIATE ABOUT MYSELF IS ___________________
____

SOMETHING I'M GRATEFUL FOR TODAY WAS _______________
____
____

DAILY DOODLE & Affirmation

SELF-CARE REFLECTIONS

DATE :   M T W T F S S

DID I SET AN INTENTION FOR THE DAY? Y / N

TODAY'S ACCOMPLISHMENTS
BIG OR SMALL

1

2

3

BODY

CUPS OF WATER DRANK: _____
HOURS SLEPT LAST NIGHT: _____
MINUTES SPENT EXERCISING: _____
WHAT I ATE TODAY NOURISHED &
ENERGIZED ME? Y / N

DIETARY NOTES: _____________
____
ONE WORD TO DESCRIBE
HOW I FELT PHYSICALLY
TODAY WAS _______________.

SOUL

DID I FEEL HOPEFUL
TODAY? Y / N
MINUTES SPENT ON
MEDITATIVE ACTIVITY OR
IN A STATE OF FLOW:

ONE THING THAT GAVE ME
PURPOSE TODAY WAS ______
____
____

SOMETHING I STRUGGLED
WITH TODAY WAS ____________
____
____

MIND

WAS MY SELF-TALK TODAY KIND
& COMPASSIONATE? Y / N

ONE THING I APPRECIATE ABOUT
MYSELF IS ______________________
____

SOMETHING I'M GRATEFUL FOR
TODAY WAS _____________________
____
____

DAILY DOODLE & Affirmation

DATE :

SELF-CARE REFLECTIONS

DATE :   M T W T F S S

DID I SET AN INTENTION FOR THE DAY? Y / N

TODAY'S ACCOMPLISHMENTS
BIG OR SMALL

1 ______
2 ______
3 ______

BODY

CUPS OF WATER DRANK: ______
HOURS SLEPT LAST NIGHT: ______
MINUTES SPENT EXERCISING: ______
WHAT I ATE TODAY NOURISHED & ENERGIZED ME? Y / N

DIETARY NOTES: ______________
____
ONE WORD TO DESCRIBE HOW I FELT PHYSICALLY TODAY WAS ____________.

SOUL

DID I FEEL HOPEFUL TODAY? Y / N
MINUTES SPENT ON MEDITATIVE ACTIVITY OR IN A STATE OF FLOW: ______

ONE THING THAT GAVE ME PURPOSE TODAY WAS ______
____
____

MIND

WAS MY SELF-TALK TODAY KIND & COMPASSIONATE? Y / N

ONE THING I APPRECIATE ABOUT MYSELF IS ______________
____

SOMETHING I'M GRATEFUL FOR TODAY WAS ______________
____
____

SOMETHING I STRUGGLED WITH TODAY WAS ____________
____
____

DAILY DOODLE & AFFIRMATION

DATE :

SELF-CARE REFLECTIONS

DATE :   M T W T F S S

DID I SET AN INTENTION FOR THE DAY? Y / N

TODAY'S ACCOMPLISHMENTS
BIG OR SMALL

1

2

3

BODY

CUPS OF WATER DRANK: _____

HOURS SLEPT LAST NIGHT: _____

MINUTES SPENT EXERCISING: _____

WHAT I ATE TODAY NOURISHED & ENERGIZED ME? Y / N

DIETARY NOTES: ____________

____

ONE WORD TO DESCRIBE HOW I FELT PHYSICALLY TODAY WAS ______________.

SOUL

DID I FEEL HOPEFUL TODAY? Y / N

MINUTES SPENT ON MEDITATIVE ACTIVITY OR IN A STATE OF FLOW: _____

ONE THING THAT GAVE ME PURPOSE TODAY WAS ______

____

____

SOMETHING I STRUGGLED WITH TODAY WAS ____________

____

____

MIND

WAS MY SELF-TALK TODAY KIND & COMPASSIONATE? Y / N

ONE THING I APPRECIATE ABOUT MYSELF IS ________________

____

SOMETHING I'M GRATEFUL FOR TODAY WAS ______________

____

DAILY DOODLE & AFFIRMATION

DATE :

I am passionate!

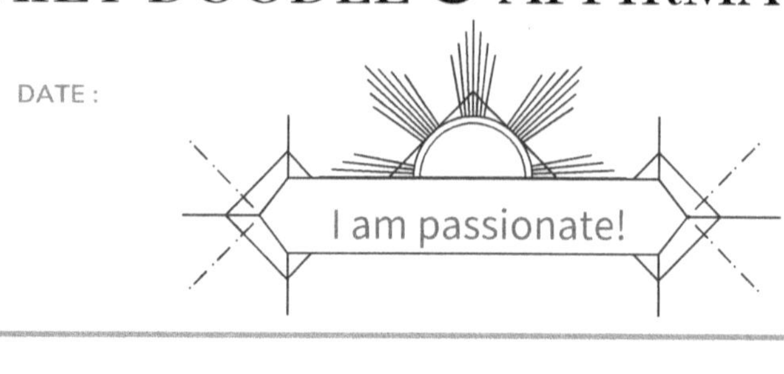

SELF-CARE REFLECTIONS

DATE: M T W T F S S

DID I SET AN INTENTION FOR THE DAY? Y / N

TODAY'S ACCOMPLISHMENTS
BIG OR SMALL

1
2
3

BODY

CUPS OF WATER DRANK: _____
HOURS SLEPT LAST NIGHT: _____
MINUTES SPENT EXERCISING: _____
WHAT I ATE TODAY NOURISHED & ENERGIZED ME? Y / N

DIETARY NOTES: ____________
____
ONE WORD TO DESCRIBE HOW I FELT PHYSICALLY TODAY WAS ____________.

SOUL

DID I FEEL HOPEFUL TODAY? Y / N
MINUTES SPENT ON MEDITATIVE ACTIVITY OR IN A STATE OF FLOW: _____

ONE THING THAT GAVE ME PURPOSE TODAY WAS _____
____
____

SOMETHING I STRUGGLED WITH TODAY WAS ____________
____
____

MIND

WAS MY SELF-TALK TODAY KIND & COMPASSIONATE? Y / N

ONE THING I APPRECIATE ABOUT MYSELF IS ____________
____

SOMETHING I'M GRATEFUL FOR TODAY WAS ____________
____
____

DAILY DOODLE & Affirmation

SELF-CARE REFLECTIONS

DATE : ___________________   M T W T F S S

DID I SET AN INTENTION FOR THE DAY? Y / N

TODAY'S ACCOMPLISHMENTS
BIG OR SMALL

1 _______________________
2 _______________________
3 _______________________

BODY

CUPS OF WATER DRANK: _____
HOURS SLEPT LAST NIGHT: _____
MINUTES SPENT EXERCISING: _____
WHAT I ATE TODAY NOURISHED & ENERGIZED ME? Y / N

DIETARY NOTES: ___________
____
ONE WORD TO DESCRIBE HOW I FELT PHYSICALLY TODAY WAS ___________.

SOUL

DID I FEEL HOPEFUL TODAY? Y / N
MINUTES SPENT ON MEDITATIVE ACTIVITY OR IN A STATE OF FLOW: _____

ONE THING THAT GAVE ME PURPOSE TODAY WAS _______
____
____

SOMETHING I STRUGGLED WITH TODAY WAS ___________
____
____

MIND

WAS MY SELF-TALK TODAY KIND & COMPASSIONATE? Y / N

ONE THING I APPRECIATE ABOUT MYSELF IS ___________________
____

SOMETHING I'M GRATEFUL FOR TODAY WAS ________________
____
____

DAILY DOODLE & AFFIRMATION

DATE :

I achieve my goals!

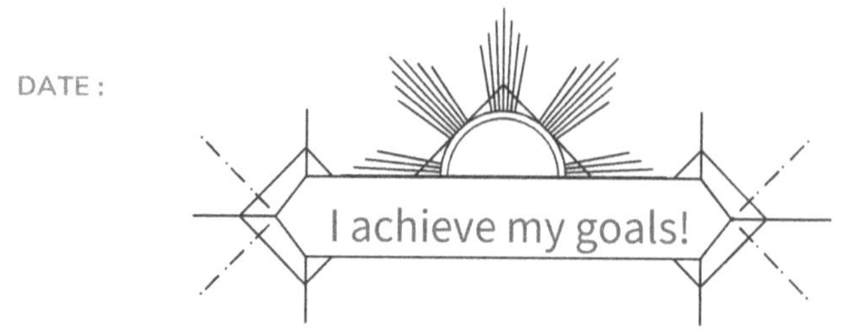

SELF-CARE REFLECTIONS

DATE: _______________   M T W T F S S

DID I SET AN INTENTION FOR THE DAY? Y / N

____

____

____

TODAY'S ACCOMPLISHMENTS
BIG OR SMALL

1 _______________________________

2 _______________________________

3 _______________________________

BODY

CUPS OF WATER DRANK: _____

HOURS SLEPT LAST NIGHT: _____

MINUTES SPENT EXERCISING: _____

WHAT I ATE TODAY NOURISHED & ENERGIZED ME? Y / N

DIETARY NOTES: _____________

____

ONE WORD TO DESCRIBE HOW I FELT PHYSICALLY TODAY WAS ____________.

SOUL

DID I FEEL HOPEFUL TODAY? Y / N

MINUTES SPENT ON MEDITATIVE ACTIVITY OR IN A STATE OF FLOW: _____

ONE THING THAT GAVE ME PURPOSE TODAY WAS ______

____

____

SOMETHING I STRUGGLED WITH TODAY WAS ___________

____

____

MIND

WAS MY SELF-TALK TODAY KIND & COMPASSIONATE? Y / N

ONE THING I APPRECIATE ABOUT MYSELF IS _______________

____

SOMETHING I'M GRATEFUL FOR TODAY WAS _______________

____

____

DAILY DOODLE & AFFIRMATION

DATE :

SELF-CARE REFLECTIONS

DATE : _______________________ M T W T F S S

DID I SET AN INTENTION FOR THE DAY? Y / N

TODAY'S ACCOMPLISHMENTS
BIG OR SMALL

1
2
3

BODY

CUPS OF WATER DRANK: _____
HOURS SLEPT LAST NIGHT: _____
MINUTES SPENT EXERCISING: _____
WHAT I ATE TODAY NOURISHED &
ENERGIZED ME? Y / N

DIETARY NOTES: ______________
____
ONE WORD TO DESCRIBE
HOW I FELT PHYSICALLY
TODAY WAS ________________.

SOUL

DID I FEEL HOPEFUL
TODAY? Y / N
MINUTES SPENT ON
MEDITATIVE ACTIVITY OR
IN A STATE OF FLOW: _____

ONE THING THAT GAVE ME
PURPOSE TODAY WAS ______
____
____

SOMETHING I STRUGGLED
WITH TODAY WAS ___________
____
____

MIND

WAS MY SELF-TALK TODAY KIND
& COMPASSIONATE? Y / N

ONE THING I APPRECIATE ABOUT
MYSELF IS _____________________
____

SOMETHING I'M GRATEFUL FOR
TODAY WAS ____________________
____
____

DAILY DOODLE & Affirmation

DATE :

SELF-CARE REFLECTIONS

DATE : ________________________ M T W T F S S

DID I SET AN INTENTION FOR THE DAY? Y / N

TODAY'S ACCOMPLISHMENTS
BIG OR SMALL

1 ________________________
2 ________________________
3 ________________________

BODY

CUPS OF WATER DRANK: _______
HOURS SLEPT LAST NIGHT: _______
MINUTES SPENT EXERCISING: _______
WHAT I ATE TODAY NOURISHED & ENERGIZED ME? Y / N

DIETARY NOTES: ____________
____
ONE WORD TO DESCRIBE HOW I FELT PHYSICALLY TODAY WAS ______________.

SOUL

DID I FEEL HOPEFUL TODAY? Y / N
MINUTES SPENT ON MEDITATIVE ACTIVITY OR IN A STATE OF FLOW: _______

ONE THING THAT GAVE ME PURPOSE TODAY WAS _______
____
____

SOMETHING I STRUGGLED WITH TODAY WAS ____________
____
____

MIND

WAS MY SELF-TALK TODAY KIND & COMPASSIONATE? Y / N

ONE THING I APPRECIATE ABOUT MYSELF IS __________________
____

SOMETHING I'M GRATEFUL FOR TODAY WAS __________________
____
____

DAILY DOODLE & AFFIRMATION

DATE :

SELF-CARE REFLECTIONS

DATE : M T W T F S S

DID I SET AN INTENTION FOR THE DAY? Y / N

TODAY'S ACCOMPLISHMENTS
BIG OR SMALL

1

2

3

BODY

CUPS OF WATER DRANK: _____
HOURS SLEPT LAST NIGHT: _____
MINUTES SPENT EXERCISING: _____
WHAT I ATE TODAY NOURISHED & ENERGIZED ME? Y / N

DIETARY NOTES: ___________
____
ONE WORD TO DESCRIBE HOW I FELT PHYSICALLY TODAY WAS ________________.

SOUL

DID I FEEL HOPEFUL TODAY? Y / N
MINUTES SPENT ON MEDITATIVE ACTIVITY OR IN A STATE OF FLOW: _____

ONE THING THAT GAVE ME PURPOSE TODAY WAS ______
____
____

SOMETHING I STRUGGLED WITH TODAY WAS ___________
____
____

MIND

WAS MY SELF-TALK TODAY KIND & COMPASSIONATE? Y / N

ONE THING I APPRECIATE ABOUT MYSELF IS ________________
____

SOMETHING I'M GRATEFUL FOR TODAY WAS ________________
____
____

DAILY DOODLE & Affirmation

SELF-CARE REFLECTIONS

DATE : M T W T F S S

DID I SET AN INTENTION FOR THE DAY? Y / N

TODAY'S ACCOMPLISHMENTS
BIG OR SMALL

1

2

3

BODY

CUPS OF WATER DRANK: _____
HOURS SLEPT LAST NIGHT: _____
MINUTES SPENT EXERCISING: _____
WHAT I ATE TODAY NOURISHED &
ENERGIZED ME? Y / N

DIETARY NOTES: ____________
____
ONE WORD TO DESCRIBE
HOW I FELT PHYSICALLY
TODAY WAS _______________.

SOUL

DID I FEEL HOPEFUL
TODAY? Y / N
MINUTES SPENT ON
MEDITATIVE ACTIVITY OR
IN A STATE OF FLOW: _____

ONE THING THAT GAVE ME
PURPOSE TODAY WAS _____
____
____

SOMETHING I STRUGGLED
WITH TODAY WAS ___________
____
____

MIND

WAS MY SELF-TALK TODAY KIND
& COMPASSIONATE? Y / N

ONE THING I APPRECIATE ABOUT
MYSELF IS _____________________
____

SOMETHING I'M GRATEFUL FOR
TODAY WAS __________________
____
____

DAILY DOODLE & AFFIRMATION

DATE :

SELF-CARE REFLECTIONS

DATE :   M T W T F S S

DID I SET AN INTENTION FOR THE DAY? Y / N

TODAY'S ACCOMPLISHMENTS
BIG OR SMALL

1

2

3

BODY

CUPS OF WATER DRANK: _____
HOURS SLEPT LAST NIGHT: _____
MINUTES SPENT EXERCISING: _____
WHAT I ATE TODAY NOURISHED &
ENERGIZED ME? Y / N

DIETARY NOTES: ___________
____
ONE WORD TO DESCRIBE
HOW I FELT PHYSICALLY
TODAY WAS _______________.

SOUL

DID I FEEL HOPEFUL
TODAY? Y / N
MINUTES SPENT ON
MEDITATIVE ACTIVITY OR
IN A STATE OF FLOW: _____

ONE THING THAT GAVE ME
PURPOSE TODAY WAS _____
____
____

SOMETHING I STRUGGLED
WITH TODAY WAS __________
____
____

MIND

WAS MY SELF-TALK TODAY KIND
& COMPASSIONATE? Y / N

ONE THING I APPRECIATE ABOUT
MYSELF IS _______________
____

SOMETHING I'M GRATEFUL FOR
TODAY WAS _______________
____
____

DAILY DOODLE & AFFIRMATION

DATE :

SELF-CARE REFLECTIONS

DATE : _______________________   M T W T F S S

DID I SET AN INTENTION FOR THE DAY? Y / N

TODAY'S ACCOMPLISHMENTS
BIG OR SMALL

1 _______________________________
2 _______________________________
3 _______________________________

BODY

CUPS OF WATER DRANK: _____
HOURS SLEPT LAST NIGHT: _____
MINUTES SPENT EXERCISING: _____
WHAT I ATE TODAY NOURISHED &
ENERGIZED ME? Y / N

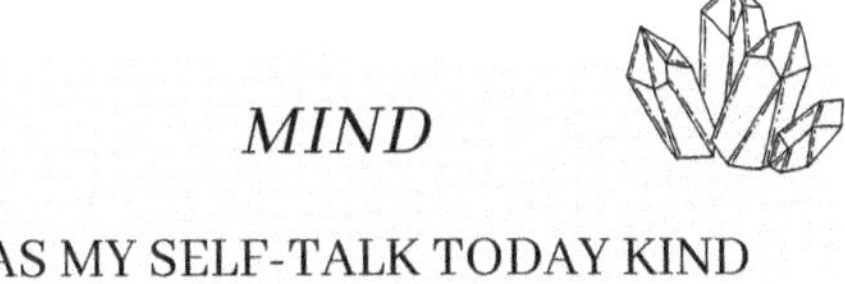

DIETARY NOTES: _____________
____
ONE WORD TO DESCRIBE
HOW I FELT PHYSICALLY
TODAY WAS _______________.

SOUL

DID I FEEL HOPEFUL
TODAY? Y / N
MINUTES SPENT ON
MEDITATIVE ACTIVITY OR
IN A STATE OF FLOW: _____

ONE THING THAT GAVE ME
PURPOSE TODAY WAS ______
____
____

SOMETHING I STRUGGLED
WITH TODAY WAS ___________
____
____

MIND

WAS MY SELF-TALK TODAY KIND
& COMPASSIONATE? Y / N

ONE THING I APPRECIATE ABOUT
MYSELF IS ____________________
____

SOMETHING I'M GRATEFUL FOR
TODAY WAS ___________________
____
____

DAILY DOODLE & AFFIRMATION

DATE :

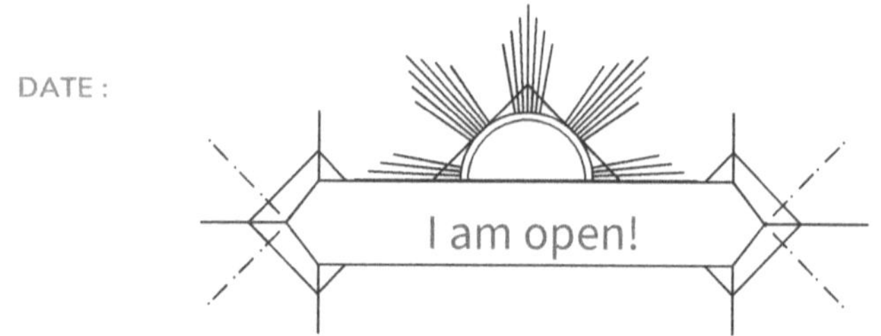

SELF-CARE REFLECTIONS

DATE :   M T W T F S S

DID I SET AN INTENTION FOR THE DAY? Y / N

TODAY'S ACCOMPLISHMENTS
BIG OR SMALL

1
2
3

BODY

CUPS OF WATER DRANK: ____
HOURS SLEPT LAST NIGHT: ____
MINUTES SPENT EXERCISING: ____
WHAT I ATE TODAY NOURISHED & ENERGIZED ME? Y / N

DIETARY NOTES: __________
____
ONE WORD TO DESCRIBE HOW I FELT PHYSICALLY TODAY WAS ____________.

SOUL

DID I FEEL HOPEFUL TODAY? Y / N
MINUTES SPENT ON MEDITATIVE ACTIVITY OR IN A STATE OF FLOW: ____

ONE THING THAT GAVE ME PURPOSE TODAY WAS ______
____
____

SOMETHING I STRUGGLED WITH TODAY WAS __________
____
____

MIND

WAS MY SELF-TALK TODAY KIND & COMPASSIONATE? Y / N

ONE THING I APPRECIATE ABOUT MYSELF IS ________________
____

SOMETHING I'M GRATEFUL FOR TODAY WAS ______________
____
____

DAILY DOODLE & AFFIRMATION

DATE :

I am whole!

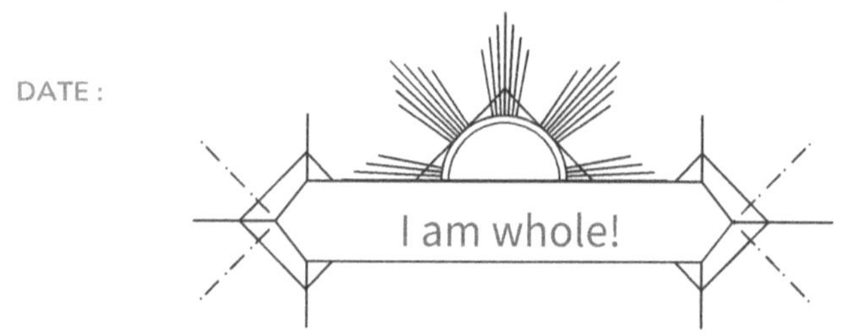

SELF-CARE REFLECTIONS

DATE :   M T W T F S S

DID I SET AN INTENTION FOR THE DAY? Y / N

TODAY'S ACCOMPLISHMENTS
BIG OR SMALL

1

2

3

BODY

CUPS OF WATER DRANK: _____

HOURS SLEPT LAST NIGHT: _____

MINUTES SPENT EXERCISING: _____

WHAT I ATE TODAY NOURISHED & ENERGIZED ME? Y / N

DIETARY NOTES: ____________

____

ONE WORD TO DESCRIBE HOW I FELT PHYSICALLY TODAY WAS ______________.

SOUL

DID I FEEL HOPEFUL TODAY? Y / N

MINUTES SPENT ON MEDITATIVE ACTIVITY OR IN A STATE OF FLOW: _____

ONE THING THAT GAVE ME PURPOSE TODAY WAS ______
____
____

MIND

WAS MY SELF-TALK TODAY KIND & COMPASSIONATE? Y / N

ONE THING I APPRECIATE ABOUT MYSELF IS ____________________
____

SOMETHING I'M GRATEFUL FOR TODAY WAS ____________________
____
____

SOMETHING I STRUGGLED WITH TODAY WAS ____________
____
____

DAILY DOODLE & AFFIRMATION

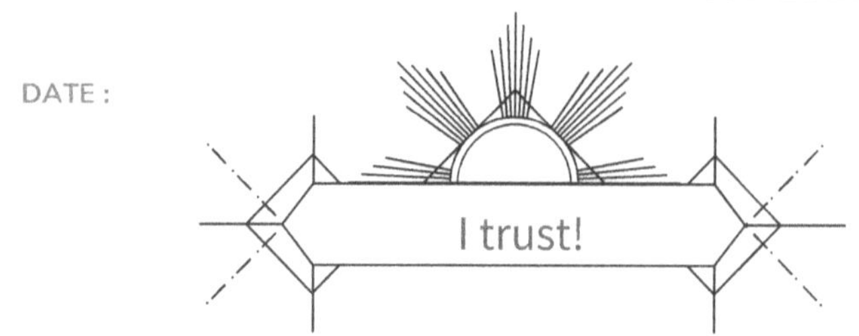

SELF-CARE REFLECTIONS

DATE :   M T W T F S S

DID I SET AN INTENTION FOR THE DAY? Y / N

TODAY'S ACCOMPLISHMENTS
BIG OR SMALL

1

2

3

BODY

CUPS OF WATER DRANK: _____

HOURS SLEPT LAST NIGHT: _____

MINUTES SPENT EXERCISING: _____

WHAT I ATE TODAY NOURISHED & ENERGIZED ME? Y / N

DIETARY NOTES: _____________

____

ONE WORD TO DESCRIBE HOW I FELT PHYSICALLY TODAY WAS ______________.

SOUL

DID I FEEL HOPEFUL TODAY? Y / N

MINUTES SPENT ON MEDITATIVE ACTIVITY OR IN A STATE OF FLOW: _____

ONE THING THAT GAVE ME PURPOSE TODAY WAS ______

____

____

SOMETHING I STRUGGLED WITH TODAY WAS ____________

____

____

MIND

WAS MY SELF-TALK TODAY KIND & COMPASSIONATE? Y / N

ONE THING I APPRECIATE ABOUT MYSELF IS ____________________

____

SOMETHING I'M GRATEFUL FOR TODAY WAS ________________

____

____

DAILY DOODLE & Affirmation

DATE :

SELF-CARE REFLECTIONS

DATE :   M T W T F S S

DID I SET AN INTENTION FOR THE DAY? Y / N

TODAY'S ACCOMPLISHMENTS
BIG OR SMALL

1

2

3

BODY

CUPS OF WATER DRANK: _____

HOURS SLEPT LAST NIGHT: _____

MINUTES SPENT EXERCISING: _____

WHAT I ATE TODAY NOURISHED & ENERGIZED ME? Y / N

DIETARY NOTES: ____________

____

ONE WORD TO DESCRIBE HOW I FELT PHYSICALLY TODAY WAS ______________.

SOUL

DID I FEEL HOPEFUL TODAY? Y / N

MINUTES SPENT ON MEDITATIVE ACTIVITY OR IN A STATE OF FLOW: _____

ONE THING THAT GAVE ME PURPOSE TODAY WAS ______

____

____

SOMETHING I STRUGGLED WITH TODAY WAS ____________

____

____

MIND

WAS MY SELF-TALK TODAY KIND & COMPASSIONATE? Y / N

ONE THING I APPRECIATE ABOUT MYSELF IS _____________________

____

SOMETHING I'M GRATEFUL FOR TODAY WAS _________________

____

____

DAILY DOODLE & AFFIRMATION

DATE :

I am a good mom!

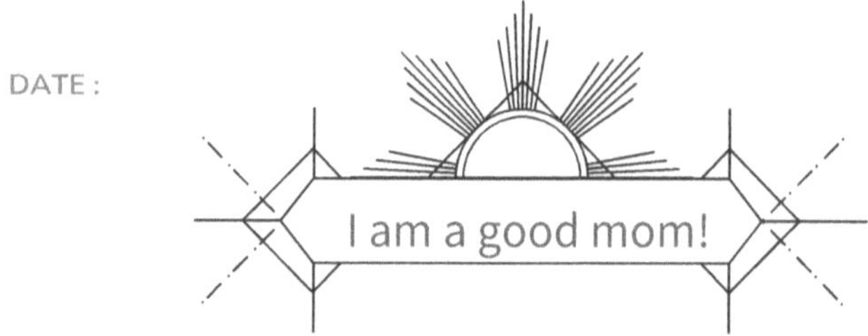

SELF-CARE REFLECTIONS

DATE :   M T W T F S S

DID I SET AN INTENTION FOR THE DAY? Y / N

TODAY'S ACCOMPLISHMENTS
BIG OR SMALL

1

2

3

BODY

CUPS OF WATER DRANK: ____

HOURS SLEPT LAST NIGHT: ____

MINUTES SPENT EXERCISING: ____

WHAT I ATE TODAY NOURISHED & ENERGIZED ME? Y / N

DIETARY NOTES: ____________
____

ONE WORD TO DESCRIBE HOW I FELT PHYSICALLY TODAY WAS _______________.

SOUL

DID I FEEL HOPEFUL TODAY? Y / N

MINUTES SPENT ON MEDITATIVE ACTIVITY OR IN A STATE OF FLOW: _____

ONE THING THAT GAVE ME PURPOSE TODAY WAS ______
____
____

SOMETHING I STRUGGLED WITH TODAY WAS ___________
____
____

MIND

WAS MY SELF-TALK TODAY KIND & COMPASSIONATE? Y / N

ONE THING I APPRECIATE ABOUT MYSELF IS ____________________
____

SOMETHING I'M GRATEFUL FOR TODAY WAS ________________
____
____

DAILY DOODLE & AFFIRMATION

DATE :

SELF-CARE REFLECTIONS

DID I SET AN INTENTION FOR
THE DAY? Y / N

TODAY'S ACCOMPLISHMENTS
BIG OR SMALL

1
2
3

BODY

CUPS OF WATER DRANK: _____
HOURS SLEPT LAST NIGHT: _____
MINUTES SPENT EXERCISING: _____
WHAT I ATE TODAY NOURISHED &
ENERGIZED ME? Y / N

DIETARY NOTES: ____________
____
ONE WORD TO DESCRIBE
HOW I FELT PHYSICALLY
TODAY WAS ______________.

SOUL

DID I FEEL HOPEFUL
TODAY? Y / N
MINUTES SPENT ON
MEDITATIVE ACTIVITY OR
IN A STATE OF FLOW: _____

ONE THING THAT GAVE ME
PURPOSE TODAY WAS ______
____
____

SOMETHING I STRUGGLED
WITH TODAY WAS ___________
____
____

MIND

WAS MY SELF-TALK TODAY KIND
& COMPASSIONATE? Y / N

ONE THING I APPRECIATE ABOUT
MYSELF IS ___________________
____

SOMETHING I'M GRATEFUL FOR
TODAY WAS ___________________
____
____

DAILY DOODLE & AFFIRMATION

DATE :

SELF-CARE REFLECTIONS

DATE :   M T W T F S S

DID I SET AN INTENTION FOR THE DAY? Y / N

TODAY'S ACCOMPLISHMENTS
BIG OR SMALL

1
2
3

BODY

CUPS OF WATER DRANK: ____

HOURS SLEPT LAST NIGHT: ____

MINUTES SPENT EXERCISING: ____

WHAT I ATE TODAY NOURISHED & ENERGIZED ME? Y / N

DIETARY NOTES: __________

____

ONE WORD TO DESCRIBE HOW I FELT PHYSICALLY TODAY WAS ____________.

SOUL

DID I FEEL HOPEFUL TODAY? Y / N

MINUTES SPENT ON MEDITATIVE ACTIVITY OR IN A STATE OF FLOW: ____

ONE THING THAT GAVE ME PURPOSE TODAY WAS _____

____

____

SOMETHING I STRUGGLED WITH TODAY WAS ___________

____

____

MIND

WAS MY SELF-TALK TODAY KIND & COMPASSIONATE? Y / N

ONE THING I APPRECIATE ABOUT MYSELF IS __________________

____

SOMETHING I'M GRATEFUL FOR TODAY WAS ________________

____

____

DAILY DOODLE & AFFIRMATION

DATE :

SELF-CARE REFLECTIONS

DATE : ________________________ M T W T F S S

DID I SET AN INTENTION FOR THE DAY? Y / N

TODAY'S ACCOMPLISHMENTS
BIG OR SMALL

1 ________________________
2 ________________________
3 ________________________

BODY

CUPS OF WATER DRANK: _____
HOURS SLEPT LAST NIGHT: _____
MINUTES SPENT EXERCISING: _____
WHAT I ATE TODAY NOURISHED & ENERGIZED ME? Y / N

DIETARY NOTES: ____________
____
ONE WORD TO DESCRIBE HOW I FELT PHYSICALLY TODAY WAS ________________.

SOUL

DID I FEEL HOPEFUL TODAY? Y / N
MINUTES SPENT ON MEDITATIVE ACTIVITY OR IN A STATE OF FLOW: _____

ONE THING THAT GAVE ME PURPOSE TODAY WAS _____
____
____

SOMETHING I STRUGGLED WITH TODAY WAS ____________
____
____

MIND

WAS MY SELF-TALK TODAY KIND & COMPASSIONATE? Y / N

ONE THING I APPRECIATE ABOUT MYSELF IS ____________________
____

SOMETHING I'M GRATEFUL FOR TODAY WAS ________________
____
____

DAILY DOODLE & AFFIRMATION

DATE :

SELF-CARE REFLECTIONS

DATE: _______________   M T W T F S S

DID I SET AN INTENTION FOR THE DAY? Y / N

TODAY'S ACCOMPLISHMENTS
BIG OR SMALL

1
2
3

BODY

CUPS OF WATER DRANK: _______
HOURS SLEPT LAST NIGHT: _______
MINUTES SPENT EXERCISING: _______
WHAT I ATE TODAY NOURISHED & ENERGIZED ME? Y / N

DIETARY NOTES: ______________
____
ONE WORD TO DESCRIBE HOW I FELT PHYSICALLY TODAY WAS ______________.

SOUL

DID I FEEL HOPEFUL TODAY? Y / N
MINUTES SPENT ON MEDITATIVE ACTIVITY OR IN A STATE OF FLOW: _______

ONE THING THAT GAVE ME PURPOSE TODAY WAS _______
____
____

SOMETHING I STRUGGLED WITH TODAY WAS ____________
____
____

MIND

WAS MY SELF-TALK TODAY KIND & COMPASSIONATE? Y / N

ONE THING I APPRECIATE ABOUT MYSELF IS __________________
____

SOMETHING I'M GRATEFUL FOR TODAY WAS ______________
____
____

NOTES:

NOTES:

NOTES:

NOTES:

DAILY DOODLE DIRECTIVES:

1. Draw your happy place.

2. Portray your dominant emotion from the day using line, shape, and/or color.

3. Draw a goal or dream for yourself.

4. Draw a big heart. Inside write or depict what fills your heart.

5. Draw a good luck charm. Recall a time you felt lucky?

6. Draw a volcano. Underneath it depict or write what makes you boil or want to erupt.

7. Draw a thought bubble. What things fill up your mind?

8. Draw your favorite food or drink. Connect to your senses.

9. Make a mask. If you wore a mask, what would it look like?

10. Draw yourself as a superhero. What is your superpower?

11. Draw your favorite animal doing something cute.

12. Draw an ocean or a wave. Reflect on when you feel in flow?

13. Create a family shield. What's most important to you and to your family?

14. Draw yourself as a tree. Imagine your strong roots.

15. Create a logo for yourself. What is your brand?

16. What does peace look like to you?

17. Depict your higher self in shape, color, line, form / what might your essence look like?

18. Create a body map. Where do you feel good and where do you feel not so good?

19. Draw a mountaintop. What makes you feel a sense of being on top and accomplishment?

20. Make a dream home. How could you make your own home more like that?

21. What does your perfect day look like?

22. Draw your favorite relaxing pastime or hobby.

23. What would your energy from today look like in shape, color, line, and /or form?

24. If you were an animal what would you be?

25. Create a monster. What is your biggest fear or scary place?

26. What does your calm look like?

27. What does your anxiety look like?

28. Design a T-shirt or outfit for yourself.

29. Draw a safe place.

30. Make a fun pattern. Reflect on some of your own day-to-day patterns.

31. Make a mini collage that represents you.

32. Depict one of your favorite childhood memories.

33. Draw a vision you have for your future? (could be tomorrow, next year, five years, 20 years from now)

34. Depict something that makes you proud.

35. What does freedom look like to you?

36. Draw a bridge. Recall a time you successfully made it through a big change or transition.

37. Draw a universe. Reflect on how big and small we all are.

38. Make a flower or plant. Think about how much you've grown as a Mom and person.

39. Create a mandala. Feel your zen.

40. Draw a book cover for your own life.

41. Design a postcard that describes you.

42. Think of something that bothers you. Draw or write it on a balloon and imagine it floating away.

43. Make a fun scribble drawing and see where it takes you. Enjoy the lack of planning and let go of control.

44. Create a wheel of emotion (make a circle and depict which primary emotions you felt today).

45. Think up and draw a wild invention that would make your life easier.

46. Make a prayer flag. What do you pray for?

47. Draw images of your strengths or positive traits.

48. Make a short fairy tale about yourself.

49. Draw an anchor. What makes you feel anchored in life?

50. Trace your hand. Depict, write, or draw how you help others inside the hand.

51. Make a window. What view would you like to see?

52. Create blocks of color (use ones that calm you).

53. Make a zentangle. Appreciate the beauty in organic spontaneity.

54. Make art based on a favorite quote, song lyric, or poem.

55. Use your non-dominant hand to doodle. Embrace the imperfection.

56. Make yourself a "permission slip." Give yourself an out for something you don't want to do or allow yourself permission to do something you'd like to do.

57. Draw a unique image representing who you love most. Who is your rock?

58. Draw a large cloud and on it depict a loss you've experienced.

59. Make a family bouquet. Depict each family member as a flower. What makes each member special?

60. Make a small portrait of your past, current, and future self. How have you changed and how do you think you will continue to transform?

61. Draw a road and on it depict something you'd like to forgive.

62. Depict your thoughts riding by on a moving train.

63. Make a hot air balloon and think of a place you'd like to visit someday.

64. Draw a butterfly. On one wing depict something you can't change. On the other wing depict something you can change.

65. Draw a picture or write a brief note for your future self.

66. Create a large sun. Inside the sun write or draw something that brings you light or that you are grateful for.

YOUR JOURNEY CONTINUES HERE.

Everything you need is where you are.